Telos,

Dreams,

and
our continuing

Human Evolution

Marley Sheng-Cecilio

Peace, Prosperity, and Today Series: Book One
July 20, 2021

Telos, Dreams, and our continuing Human Evolution
Copyright © 2021 by Marley Sheng-Cecilio

All rights reserved. No part of this publication may be reproduced, distributed, or transmitted in any form or by any means, including photocopying, recording, or other electronic or mechanical methods, without the prior written permission of the publisher or author, except in the case of brief quotations embodied in critical reviews and certain other noncommercial uses permitted by copyright law.

Although every precaution has been taken to verify the accuracy of the information contained herein, the author and publisher assume no responsibility for any errors or omissions. No liability is assumed for damages that may result from the use of information contained within.

Library of Congress Control Number: 2021913160
   ISBN-13:   Paperback: 978-1-64749-533-6
                    ePub: 978-1-64749-534-3

Printed in the United States of America

GoToPublish LLC
1-888-337-1724
www.gotopublish.com
info@gotopublish.com

For
Emmanuel, Rowena, and Ethan
Larry and Diane
Orlando, Emmeline, and Nicholas Tyler
Vered Marley

Also for
Papa Sheng Nam (Chiu Yee)
Mama Jacinta Avanzado Sheng
  & my siblings,
the 13 Shengs and their families

CONTENTS

PREFACE v

PART I
DEFINITIONS AND OVERVIEWS

Chap 1 The Telos and the Mind 3
Chap 2 Hurtful Teachings of the Intellectuals 26
Chap 3 How does Human Evolution happen? 45

PART II
CHARACTERISTICS OF THE TELOS

Chap 4 Psychic Energies and
           Invisible Particles that are not *spirit* .... .69
Chap 5 What does it feel like to be "touched" by
           the *spirit*? 80

PART III
JUNG'S PARADIGM OF INDIVIDUATION

Chap 6 Who was Carl G. Jung? ....…..101
Chap 7 Notes about Jung's Paradigm of
           Individuation 121

BIBLIOGRAPHY 128

PREFACE

In 2021, the year this book was published, personal views and experiences that are shared publicly can be scrutinized and taken apart by social media. Still, I take this risk, because many millions who are undergoing unusual dream experiences like mine, do not yet know that their unusual dream experiences *are* stages of their *continuing human evolution* to their state of completeness.

These kinds of unusual dream experiences are powerful, unstoppable, and can be overwhelming. Once they start, these upheaving and metamorphic dream experiences will continue for the rest of people's lifetime and are carried forward in their lineage.

Those fortunate ones whose dream experiences are on the right path, describe their experiences as a *religious conversion*, a *nirvana experience*, or as *amazing grace*.

Those whose dream experiences do not go well could suffer from confusion or be diagnosed with neurosis, depression, paranoia, delusions, schizophrenia, and other forms of emotional and mental disorders.

If you, the reader, intuitively relate and *know* about the experiences described in this book, then this book is for you. Like a shepherd's staff, I hope it will help guide you and your lineage, in however small a way, to journey safely to a higher state of being.

If this book will seem outlandish, I hope that you will read it anyway, so that you will become familiar with the *Telos* or *spirit*, which is the highest form of intelligence in the universe that resides in us all. It will serve you well to know about the *special dreams* that contain the symbolic roadmap and blueprint of our continuing human evolution and the *powerful instincts* that trigger and guide these processes.

PART I
DEFINITIONS AND OVERVIEWS

*... man is only now,
after a million years of existence,
emerging from his embryonic phase.*[1]

---

[1] Pierre Teilhard de Chardin, *Man's Place in Nature* (New York: Harper & Row, 1959), 116.

Chapter 1
THE TELOS and THE MIND

On the 6th Day of Creation,

> *Yahweh God planted a garden in Eden which is in the east, and there he put the man he had fashioned from the soil. Yahweh God caused to grow every kind of tree, enticing to look at and good to eat, with the* **Tree of Life** *and the* **Tree of Knowledge of Good and Evil** *in the middle of the garden.* (Gen. 2:7-10)

This book postulates that in every living thing that Yahweh God creates, He also plants seeds from the *Tree of Life* and the *Tree of Knowledge of Good and Evil*, to function as its realms of intelligence. All living things including humans, therefore, have not one, but *two* realms of intelligence.

The substance of the *Tree of Life* is *invisible* and intangible <u>spirit</u>.[2] This is why, in God's garden in Eden, the snake, Eve, and Adam did *not see* this tree, and Eve and

---

[2] Because the word "spirit" has many meanings, in this book when used as a synonym of Telos, *spirit* is italicized.

Adam were *unable* to eat its fruit. For that same reason, because it is invisible, even until today humans still do not know and are *unconscious*,[3] that the *Tree of Life* lives in them.

The *Tree of Life* which in this book is called **Telos**,[4] **spirit,** or **unconscious**, is cosmic in its scope. Humans who are *aligned* with the Telos are aligned with God's *design and purpose in Creation* and will find goodness, prosperity, joy and meaning in their existence. Those *un-aligned* with the Telos and with God's design and purpose, will experience hardships, bitterness, and emptiness.

In contrast, the substance of the *Tree of Knowledge of Good and Evil* is <u>matter</u>, which is why this tree was *visible* to the snake, Eve, and Adam. When the serpent tempted Eve with the **lie** that if they eat the fruit of this tree, they will not die; instead, their eyes will be opened, and they will know good and evil like the gods; Eve reached out for its low-lying fruit and ate it *with the* ***serpent's lie*** *in it.* She gave some to Adam who was with her, and he also ate the fruit *with the* ***serpent's lie*** *in it.* Consequently, the ***serpent's lie*** now resides permanently in every human being.

In this book, the *Tree of Knowledge of Good and Evil* in humans is called the **mind** or **consciousness**.[5] We are all familiar with our *mind* because its powers are accessible to us, and we use it every day.

---

[3] *Unconscious* is that extensive area in the psyche that is *not* in the person's immediate field of awareness and is *not* known or felt to exist.

[4] Telos is extracted from the word *teleology,* the teaching that organic life and their development can be fully explained *only* by the action of *divine design and purpose,* <u>not</u> by mechanical ways.

[5] *Consciousness* is that part of mental life of which the person *is* aware. As opposed to *unconscious*.

Our two realms of intelligence – the **Telos** and the **mind** – have different natures, powers, and functions. Because they have different natures and substances, these two realms of intelligence do not ever comingle or merge.

Both our Telos and our mind shape our behaviors, worldviews, day to day lives, and destiny. Their characteristics are described in this chapter.

THE TELOS
and its characteristics

1. **This book postulates that the *Tree of Life* which in this book is called Telos or *spirit*, is the *immortal womb* that contains all of Creation, and also the *cosmic spirit* that guides, sustains, and nurtures everything in Creation. Next to God, the highest realm of intelligence in the universe is the *Tree of Life* or Telos; <u>not</u> the human mind.**

Unlike the mind, the Telos in humans is not *cephalic*. It does *not* reside inside our cephal or head. As I have experienced it, the Telos or *spirit* functions from inside the nuclei of our billions of microscopic body cells. This is why it intimately knows every aspect of you and me.

Our Telos or *spirit* knows who we are and what we do, every moment of our waking and sleeping hours. When we dream, when we hope, when we are sad, when sitting doing nothing, and even when we are being bad, we are always *in the spirit.*

Know as well, that Telos or *spirit* is *one-piece*. The *spirit* in you is the very same *spirit* that is in me, in everyone, and in everything living and nonliving, from the dust on the ground to the single-celled bacteria, to the plants and animals, to the stars, planets, comets, and galaxies of our expanding universe.

Even beyond death, the *spirit* remains unbroken.

My older brother Jessie, whom we referred to as Nonoy, passed away in March 2019. On the 40th day after he died – which my Mama's religious traditions believe is the day when the newly dead departs from the earth and goes up to heaven – I was comforted when I dreamt of my brother. In the dream, he was looking well, smiling, and interacting with family members and friends. I felt *one-piece* with my brother *in the spirit*, even though he is now in the next life.

However, even though creation and the universe are held together as *one-piece* in the Telos – elements, creatures, and humans are *not* a big bowl of *sameness*. Each element, living thing, and human being is a complete, separate, unique, free, and autonomous **individual**! God did not create humans to look the same, think in the same way, and be equal, *equivalent* and *interchangeable* as husbands, wives, siblings, parents, children, grandchildren, and so on. God created each leaf, each squirrel, each virus, each tree, each star, and even each snowflake to be unique, complete, free, and different from every other of its kind.

Know that neither God nor the cosmic intelligence of the Telos requires that everyone must be vegetarian. Some love beef, pork, or bacon, and that is fine. It is all right that some people want to own guns and some don't. In the ups and downs of life, sometimes one is poor, and at other times rich; at times, happy and content, and at other times, angry and bitter. Life is what we make it. Within the boundaries and guidance of our nature and the teleological laws, you are free to be who you are, and I am free to be who I am.

Finally, know too, that the only place in the universe where people can find, see, and feel the *nearness* of God, where we can speak to Him as we are and ask Him for help and answers, is the realm of Telos; because like the Telos, God is also *spirit.*⁶

> **II. The Telos or *spirit* is u*nknowable* to the mind, and its substance *cannot* be *penetrated* by chemicals, human techniques, and gadgets.**
> **But the Telos permanently resides in our microscopic body cells. It is the intelligence that sustains, nourishes, and nurtures our bodily and mental functioning, development, and well-being.**

Psychology, psychiatry, and most intellectuals make it seem as though reason, science, willpower, human gadgets, and techniques have free access to every aspect of our body and inner world. *It is not so*. Unless the Telos allows it, there is no power, gadget, or technique in the universe that can force entry from the outside, into its realm. The door to the Telos, like Karl Barth's divine revelation, can only be *"unlocked from the inside."* ⁷

Nor can the realm of Telos be penetrated by hypnosis, yoga, and other psychological techniques, or tampered with by mind-altering chemicals like marijuana, opium, and cocaine.

---

⁶ The Telos and God are both invisible and immortal *spirit*. The difference between them is, that God the Creator is a *divine* and uncreated Spirit; while the Telos is not divine; it is an *"earthly"* and *"created"* spirit.

⁷ Karl Barth's definition of divine revelation: *"Divine revelation,"* Barth continues, *"cannot be discovered in the same way as the beauty of a work of art or the genius of a man is discovered.... It is the opening of a door that can **only be unlocked from the inside.**"* As quoted by Thomas Merton in his <u>Conjectures of an Innocent Bystander</u> (New York: Image Books, 2009), 10. (Bold in this footnote quote was added.)

Nor can the *spirit* be studied by quantum mechanics, smashed by atom colliders, or tweaked by bio-engineering techniques and gadgets.

Even the holiest saints or the Pope, cannot enter the realm of Telos at their personal bidding or manipulate and harness the realm of the *spirit* for their use.

Forces, powers, and substances that are matter cannot merge with, penetrate, capture, or manipulate the realm of the *spirit* in any way.

Yet it is the *spirit* that sustains, nurtures, and sustains all aspects of our brain and mind.

Because in the *spirit*, all things in creation are connected as *one-piece*, when a child, woman, or man is in dire circumstances or in deep sorrows and suffering, *instantly* the Telos feels it. Even if they do not ask for help, wherever they may be, the Telos will immediately find them, soothe them with calm, and pump them with courage and insights to help them cope and endure. When facing defeat, sorrow, pain and despair, the Telos strengthens our hope, courage, endurance, and stubbornness.

Unbeknownst to many – since time began and across all regions, races, religions, and walks of life - the Telos faithfully brings *justice* and *comfort* to "*bruised reeds,*" [8] those people who are unfairly cheated by others. I know this to be true, because as narrated in chap 3 of this book, it happened to me.

At night when we sleep, no matter what color yours and my skin is, the Telos reveals to everyone, God's guidelines, teachings, and commandments through our dreams, visions, visuals, and other extra-sensory ways.

---

[8] "... *a **bruised reed** he will not break and a smoldering wick he will not snuff out. In faithfulness **he will bring forth justice**; he will not falter nor be discouraged till he establishes justice on earth.*" (Is. 2:3; Mt. 12:20)

At rare times, God thru the Telos even intervenes in Creation with miracles, instant healing, signs, wonders, and other supernatural phenomena, to help humankind be safe and find their way in life.

What is one sign that a person is *in* the realm of the immortal Telos*?*

He or she will know because good things will begin to happen. Things will fall into place in their lives. They will feel rooted in peace, humility, truth, self-acceptance, freedom, and contentment. They will feel grounded, happy, and endowed with meaning in their lives. They will have reason to live.

III. The nature of the Telos, *spirit*, or unconscious is *religious;* <u>not</u> sexual. <u>Freud was wrong</u>.[9]

It <u>was</u> God who reached out to humans and revealed who He is when humans first appeared on earth 5 or 6 million years ago; otherwise, because God is invisible, the human race on their own could *not* have found the way to Him. To help humans survive, prosper, and not be afraid, God ongoingly blesses them with His protection, guidance, teachings, and commandments.

When God "spoke" to the women, children, and men in those early times, His words were branded like hot iron into their billions of body cells as truths, commandments, and teachings that they remembered forever.

The ancients obeyed and lived God's "*spoken words*" carefully, exactly, and scrupulously, with all their hearts, with all their minds, and with all their souls. Then they carefully and diligently compiled those knowledge,

---

[9] Chapters 2 and 6 of this book describe Freud's **grievous errors** and their devastating consequences.

commandments, teachings, and guidance received from God, into *sacred*[10] books, rites, rituals, ethical values, teachings, beliefs, moral guidelines, traditions [11] and institutions[12] that they called **religion**.[13]

For example, in India, around 15,000 B.C., the ancient Hindu sages felt the *"breath of God"* as they stood along the banks of the rivers in India. Those men and women "listened" and over many generations, they translated the *"breath of God"* that they felt, into sacred chants or songs of prayer. Those songs of prayer were orally passed on from generation to generation and became *Hinduism*, one of the oldest religions of the world.

> *Thousands of years ago, before Moses or Buddha or Christ had lived, sages stood on India's riverbanks and sang. Their songs, Hindus say, were inspired by "**the breath of God**".*

> *Out of these chants – there were more than 15,000 stanzas in the earliest collection, known as the **Rig Veda** – and out of the wisdom and the spirituality of the sages since, has grown the religion known as **Hinduism**. It is the faith of more than 300 million*[14]

---

[10] *Sacred* refers to holy objects, actions and practices that are set apart and consecrated for divinity; not to be profaned.

[11] *Traditions* are inherited, established, or customary patterns of thought, actions, or behavior handed down from one generation to another *without written instructions*.

[12] *Institutions* are established organizations or associations, *with* written instructions.

[13] *Religion* is the beliefs, attitudes, behaviors, etc. that constitute the relationship of a person or community with God and with the heavenly powers and principles of the universe.

[14] "Today it is shared by some 450 million people, most of them in India...." National Geographic Society, <u>Great Religions of the World</u> (Washington D.C: National Geographic Book Service, 1971), 36.

human beings in India and of about 15 million more elsewhere. It has influenced thoughtful men of many lands throughout the centuries. [15]

The *Rig Veda* ("knowledge of the verses"), composed in northwest India, preserved by oral tradition, and written in archaic Sanskrit between 15,000 and 12,000 B.C., is a collection of 1,017 prayers and hymns contained in 10 chapters. Below is an example of a *Veda* or chant:

In the beginning there was neither naught nor aught: Then there was neither sky nor atmosphere above... Then was there neither day, nor night, nor light, nor darkness, Only the Existent One breathed calmly, self-contained. [16]

Hinduism worships one God – *Brahman*, the eternal Spirit. Brahman, in turn, is composed of the Hindu Trinity of *Brahma* (the Creator God), *Vishnu* (protector and maintainer of world order), and *Shiva* (God of destruction and reproduction).

Vishnu and Shiva often use a human or animal identity, called an **avatar**, and descend on earth to destroy the wicked, to clarify true teachings, or restore justice and order in the world.

Krishna, for example, is an *avatar* of Vishnu. The 330 million gods and goddesses that Hinduism worships could be the *avatars* assumed by their Gods and Goddesses.

In addition to the Rig Veda, Hinduism has 2 major religious epics that contain its teachings: the *Mahabharata* ("great story of the descendants of Bharata") and the *Ramayana* ("the exploits of Rama").

---

[15] Editorial Staff of LIFE, <u>The World's Great Religions</u> (New York: Golden Press, 1967), 19. (Bold was added.)

[16] National Geographic, <u>Great Religions</u>, 34.

In the 6th Book of the Mahabharata called the *Bhagavad Gita* ("song of the glorious one"), Krishna who is an *avatar* of Vishnu, teaches the Hindus to worship him through **yoga**.

This quote from the *Bhagavad Gita* below explains that **yoga**, through its specific postures and exercises, will develop in them the capacity for *moral restraints* and also awaken *an energy* that will enable their souls to merge with their God Krishna.

From: **Bhagavad Gita**
Chapter Seven: Knowledge of the Absolute

Text 1: The Supreme Personality of Godhead said: Now hear, O son of Prtha, how by practicing **yoga** *in full consciousness of Me, with mind attached to Me, you can know Me in full, free from doubt.*

Text 2: I shall now declare unto you in full this knowledge, both phenomenal and numinous. This being known, nothing further shall remain for you to know.

Text 3: Out of many thousands among men, one may endeavor for perfection, and of those who have achieved perfection, hardly one knows Me in truth.

Text 4: Earth, water, fire, air, ether, mind, intelligence, and false ego – all together these eight constitute My separated material energies.

...

Text 30: Those in full consciousness of Me, who know Me, the Supreme Lord, to be the governing principle of the material manifestation, of the demigods, and of all methods of sacrifice, can understand and know Me, the Supreme Personality of Godhead, even at the time of death.

In the past 5 or 6 million years, God protected, taught, and guided not only the people of India, but *all* the groups of other humans living in different parts of the world, in *all* the different eras and circumstances as well. These other people also responded to God in their own and *different **religious** ways.

As an example, the people of China were also cognizant of the heavenly powers and forces in their land and in their lives. But although next-door neighbor to India, the Chinese did not form a formal religion and most of them do not worship gods and goddesses like the Hindus. The Chinese respond and honor the heavenly powers in a more abstract and philosophical way.

Centuries after the Hindus had chanted and wrote their *Rig Veda* in Sanskrit, the story goes that in 604 B.C., a sage in China named Lao Tzu left his position in the emperor's court in search for a different way of life. At a border outpost, the gatekeeper recognized Lao Tzu and pleaded with the sage to stay with the gatekeeper for a few days, to write down his thoughts and teachings; which Lao Tzu did. Then Lao Tzu left and was never heard from again.

The writings that Lao Tzu left behind were later published as the *Tao Te Ching* and his teachings which were later called *Taoism,* is the closest to what can be called a Chinese religion and philosophy.

In the opening stanza of the *Tao Te Ching* on the next page, Lao Tzu's highest power of the universe is not a god or goddess, but he named it the **Tao**, the "*Nothingness… that one can see something of … in everything.*"

Tao Te Ching[17]

The Tao that can be talked about is not the true Tao.
The name that can be named is not the eternal name.
Everything in the universe comes out of Nothing.

Nothing – the nameless, is the beginning;
While Heaven, the Mother, is the creatrix of all things.

Follow the nothingness of the Tao,
and you can be like it, not needing anything,
seeing the wonder and the root of everything.

And even if you cannot grasp this nothingness,
you can still see something of the Tao in everything.

These two are the same
only called by different names
and both are mysterious and wonderful.

All mysteries are Tao, and Heaven is their mother:
She is the gateway and the womb-door.

Expectedly, because God has been guiding, teaching, protecting, and nurturing all people in all places and circumstances for 5 or 6 million years; we would expect that in this 3rd millennium there would now be thousands of religions. Yes, we do!

There are now over 5,000 religions and sects in the world, and these religions have different names for their gods and goddesses and have different rituals, beliefs, practices, commandments, and traditions.

---

[17] Man-Ho Kwok, et. al., *Tao Te Ching: A new translation by Man-Ho Kwok, Martin Palmer, Jay Ramsay* (New York: Barnes & Noble Books, 1994), 27.

Paul Hutchison in his book *How Mankind Worships* aptly describes,

> *Man is a religious being. His religion has taken endless forms. His names for gods and goddesses are numerous beyond counting. The rituals through which he has sought protection or blessing vary from the horrible to the sublime.*[18]

These differences in the world's thousands of religions are *not* a bad thing. *It is the truth.* Because God is a living God, it was to be expected that He would look and act differently to different people, in different times, in different places, and under different circumstances. As Hinduism puts it, the 330 million deities that they worship *"are only the infinite aspects of the one Brahman."* [19]

The positive thing to keep in mind is, that **most religious people are alike** in that they value *truth, humility, goodness of heart, kindness, endurance, family life, peace, freedom, and justice.*

Most religious people are also **similarly infused** with *courage, hopefulness, the capacity to forgive,* and *the capacity to feel the nearness of their god or goddess, angels, and saints.*

Except for perhaps a handful of religions who live in hate, teach hate, and are warmongers; almost all religions are **a great controlling power** for *preventing people from breaking out destructively.*

---

[18] Paul Hutchison, "How Mankind Worships," <u>The World's Great Religions</u> (New York: Golden Press, 1954), 7.

[19] <u>World's Great Religions</u>, 19.

My Book Three, entitled *The Theology and Prophecies of my 8 Dreams*, which is planned for publication in late 2025, will attempt to show in a humble way, that the dream symbols, teachings, commandments, prophecies, and supernatural experiences of people in most religions, are all somehow correlated with the *stages of our continuing human evolution to our state of completeness*, as revealed in my 8 dreams.

IV. The Telos has the *phylogenetic* function to evolve every species in Creation, including humankind, to their state of completeness.

It may surprise most readers to know that humans, the youngest, latest, and possibly last species in Creation, are still *uncompleted creations*.

Compared to the fishes that have swam in the earth's seas for over 400 million years; the conifer trees and dragonflies that have been around for over 300 million years; and the mammals that have roamed the earth for over 200 million years; humans appeared on earth only about 5 or 6 million years ago.

The evolutionist Pierre Teilhard de Chardin, estimated that it takes 80 million years for a species to attain its state of maturity.

> *To put the depths of life into their true perspective, we had best return to… the layer of the mammal. Because this layer is relatively young, we have some idea of the time required for its development at the end of the Cretaceous period when it clearly emerges above the reptiles: the whole of the*

*Tertiary era and a little more – some **eighty million years**.*[20]

If Teilhard's estimate is close enough, we humans *as a species,* may still have 74 million more years of evolution to undergo.

Our being still toddlers in the timeline of evolution explains why we humans still *cannot* hold on to lasting happiness; *cannot* live in peace with ourselves and with each other; why we *blame other people* for our faults and failures; and why we *inflict violence* on each other when hurt, angry or frustrated.

Humankind's continuing human evolution to their state of completeness are guided by a powerful group of dreams and instincts that were **discovered,** documented, studied, and described in his writings by Carl Gustav Jung (1865-1961), a Swiss psychoanalyst. Jung's life, works, discoveries, and theories are described in Part III of this book.

THE MIND
and its characteristics

The word "mind" has been loosely used over the years and has many meanings. In this book, "mind" will refer *only* to the intelligence called *consciousness* that is produced by the brain and contained within our head or cranium.

---

[20] Pierre Teilhard de Chardin, *The Phenomenon of Man* (New York: Harper & Row, 1959), 136. (Bold was added.)

The *pre-conscious,*[21] *unconscious,* and *extra-sensory* organs, processes and powers which are *not* contained in the head, and which functionally reside in the nuclei of our body cells, are sorted with the Telos, *not with the mind.*

By reason that Freud's id-ego-superego schema and terminologies relating to the mind[22] have not been verified scientifically, Freudian terms, concepts, and theories are *not* considered in this book's characterizations of mind.

I. Because of my experiences in the *spirit* these past 34 years, I have concluded that our mind is a tremendously powerful *processor* of data and information, like the digital intelligence of a computer. It is a machine; *not* a living and autonomous intelligence like the Telos.

As we know, our 5 senses ongoingly gather data and information about objects, phenomena, and events in our world and send them to our brain. The brain in turn produces the mechanical intelligence that we call *mind* or *consciousness*.

The mind is a passing phenomenon, like the flame of burning coal. Like the digital intelligence which is *on* when the computer is on, and *off* when the computer is off; our mind is also *only on* when we are awake. It is *off* when we sleep.

If you, the reader, agrees with this writer that our mind can *only* know and understand about *visible* and *physical* objects and events that our 5 senses *can* grasp; then, you may

---

[21]*Preconscious* refer to those areas of the psyche that are not in immediate awareness but capable of being recalled readily into consciousness.

[22] Terms which Freud considered to be part of the mind include *eros, thanatos, repression, resistance, pleasure principle, oedipal conflicts, compulsion to repeat, primary process, secondary process,* etc.

also concur with this writer, that invisible and intangible objects, phenomena, and events - including our feelings, inklings, intuition, insights, dreams, visuals, prophecies, visions, drives, and instincts, etc. - which our 5 senses can*not* see, taste, smell, touch, or hear – are **unknowable** and **can*not* be understood** by the mind.

Because our mind is a machine, we should therefore not expect the mind to have autonomy. Nor expect our mind to have the capacity to be the origin and source of our thoughts. Nor expect our minds to have willpower.

We should not expect our mind to have the capacity to make us feel happy, hopeful, enduring, or brave.

Our mind can quantify but it can*not* know the *qualitative* difference between a truth and a lie.

It does not know about the invisible Telos or about the destiny that Telos has ready for humankind.

It can*not* know or find God because God is *spirit* and is invisible to our 5 senses.

Therefore, do not use your mind for moral and spiritual choices and decisions in your life. Morality, spirituality, truth, and wisdom come from the living Telos, *not from the mind*. When you feel lost or are tempted to do immoral, suicidal, or homicidal acts, turn *not* to science or your mind. Turn to the *spirit* in you and sincerely ask for guidance and help from God.

To find God, whoever and wherever you are, use your feelings, inklings, prayers and go inward into your inner world. Simply close your eyes and sincerely say; *"God, I need your help;"* or *"I'd like to know you, God."* In turn, God will respond to you. His "touch" of peace and gladness will find you, wherever you are. And He will speak to your heart through your inklings, visions, visuals, feelings, dreams, and other extra-sensory, spiritual, and supernatural pathways.

II. Our mind is mortal. It *is* subject to death.

When we die, our bodies, brain systems, mind and the contents of our mind - our knowledge, understanding, experiences, and memories - die with us.

But humankind has not felt the weighty loss and bankruptcy of death because amazingly and providentially, our primitive ancestors intuitively and with tremendous foresight, *preserved, memorialized,* and *passed on* aspects of their experiences, discoveries, and histories from generation to generation, all the way down to us.

The ancients left us drawings in caves, on stones, and papyrus. They left us Stonehenge. The pyramids. The 4,000 years old Men-an-Tol in Cornish, England, the "stone with a hole" through which a baby is passed so it can receive blessings and be protected from rickets, consumptive, or fevers. Also in England, the markings on the rocks made 4,000 years ago on which one can pour milk, oil, or blood and divine your future based on the patterns that are revealed on those markings. The ancients left us hundred millions of their treasures, discoveries, and wonders that they cherished and preserved, all over the world and under the world. How wonderful of our ancient ancestors, to have the foresight and goodness of heart to want to pass on to us, all their treasures and learnings.

As a result, because our primitive ancestors diligently and orally taught and passed on their songs, poetry, myths, stories, laws, prayers, beliefs, fishing gears, dances, burial rituals, wisdom, customs, and knowledge as **traditions** and **legacies** from parents to children, through 5 or 6 million years down to the modern times, except for its sadness, the human race were not overburdened by the terminal aspects of death.

Modern humans have continued this ancient practice of recording, memorializing, and passing on our knowledge, adaptations, accomplishments, and yearnings as **legacies**;[23] in the form of books and as architecture, statues, churches, monuments, songs, dances, stories, myths, and so on.

As will be described in great detail in my Book Two, these **legacies** from the ancient times are *irreplaceable* and *precious* because they are *one-of-a-kind* symbolic and physical documentations of the *concrete truths* about our history and development *as a species;* they embody the core beliefs, values, ideals, prophecies, and teachings that have made our species human. If these legacies are lost or destroyed, humanity will not know who they are, where they came from, and where they are going.

These *legacies* also appear in people's dreams. If humanity is no longer in touch with their religions, cultural and moral traditions; or have destroyed their *legacies*, then they will no longer understand the symbols in their dreams and the prophecies. They will have no roadmaps to guide them to their state of completion.

In 2020 however, just last year, in a few states in the U.S., some rioters and protesters disdained and vowed to destroy **statues**, **monuments**, and other **legacies** as pay back for alleged past injustices done to their ancestors on account of race.

But these *legacies* which took many thousands of generations to build, are not for or against any person, race, or religion. They are the story of our human civilization; where we have been and where we *should* be going.

Preserving our legacies, traditions and institutions is the way by which humans can overcome the limitations of death, the limitations of our minds, and it ensures that the symbolic maps of our continuing evolution are preserved for generations to come.

---

[23] A *legacy* is something received from an ancestor or predecessor or from the past.

Moderns, millennials, and those who come after us, must respect, understand, and cherish our *legacies, histories, moral and cultural traditions*, and *prophecies*.

III. It is our *ego* that makes our decisions and judgments, **not** the mind.

People often say, "My mind is made up." But our mind does not think or make decisions. The mind is a data processor, not a living and autonomous intelligence.

It is our **ego**, the centeredness in us that we call "*I*" or "*me*," that makes our judgment and decisions.
"**I** will go here, not there"
"**I** will not go." Or,
"**I** will go later."

This drawing on the right shows the symbolic position of the **ego** at the **center** of the mind, to indicate that our **ego** is the sovereign power that rules over the mind.

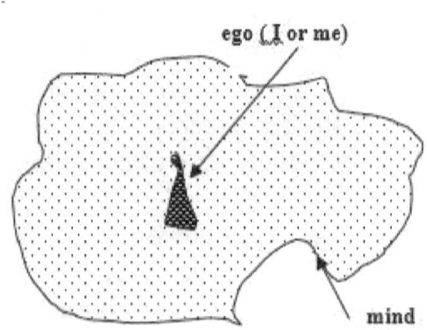

Fig. 1.1 The ego rules the mind

Per Carl Jung,
> *No consciousness can exist without a subject, that is, an **ego** to which the contents are related. Consciousness needs a center, an **ego** to which something is conscious. We know of no other kind of consciousness, nor can we imagine a consciousness without an **ego**. There can be no consciousness when there is no one to say, "I am conscious."* [24]

---

[24] Carl G. Jung, <u>*The Archetypes of the Collective Unconscious*</u>. Vol 9, Part I of *Collected Works* (New Jersey: Princeton University Press, 1969), 283. (Bold was added.)

Until we humans are more grown up and mature, we must *all* be **extremely thoughtful, restrained**, and **cautious** with our *judgments*, *decisions*, and *behaviors*. Keep in mind that ultimately, it is **our ego** that makes all our decisions and judgments; and **our ego is still a mere child** in the timeline of evolution.

IV. Our mind is the only place in the universe where the s*erpent's lie* resides permanently.

Nowhere else in Creation does the *serpent's lie* exist except in the minds of humans. We humans are the only creatures in the universe who *lie* to each other and to ourselves. Wherever we humans exist, the *serpent's lie* also exists with us.

We ourselves and the *serpent's lie* in us are the **cause** of wars, envy, murders, anger, divisiveness, immorality, suicides, bribery, arrogance, double-standards, betrayals, injustice, turmoil, and of the breakdown of friendships, family ties, marriages, governments, and civilizations.

Fortuitously, just as the *serpent's lie* resides permanently inside our minds, so also, truth, beauty, justice, peace, harmony, and the *nearness* of God permanently reside in our Telos or *spirit*.

Every night when we sleep, like a good father, the Telos sorts the anxieties, doubts, fears, and other woes inside our mind or consciousness, and provides answers and nurturance where needed. So that every morning, we wake up refreshed and ready to take up the challenges of the next day.

Our consciousness, Jung explained, does not create itself or its contents. Like the earth that does not create its own light, the contents of our consciousness or mind, is ongoingly created and recreated by our unconscious or Telos.

> *... indeed our consciousness does not support itself – it wells up from unknown depths. In childhood it awakens gradually, and all through life it wakes up each morning out of the depths of sleep from an unconscious condition. It is like a child that is born daily out of the primordial womb of the unconscious.*[25]

Therefore, as long as we humans <u>*allow* our minds and egos to *receive*</u> nourishment and guidance from our Telos or *spirit;* from our family systems; from moral and cultural traditions; and from our churches and religious institutions, ongoingly and consistently; the Telos <u>*will protect*</u> us and <u>*will revoke* the serpent's lies</u> residing in our minds!

***That* <u>was</u> the way it <u>*was*</u>,** for millions of years! For as long as humans trusted in God and in the Telos in them and they were God's people - no matter what hardships and suffering our ancestors encountered in the world, humans robustly burgeoned, evolved, and *thrived* in amazing ways!

As proof, think back to 200,000 years ago when humans may have been living in caves or in open fields and had *no formal language* yet. Like other creatures, they probably grunted and gestured to communicate with each other.

But look at us today!

---

[25] Carl G. Jung, <u>*Psychology and Religion: West and East,*</u> Vol. 11 of CW (New Jersey: Princeton University Press), 59, as quoted in the Glossary of <u>*Memories, Dreams, Reflections,*</u> 394.

After humans learned to build fires, make tools, developed cooperative hunting techniques, began to eat meat, practiced deliberate burial; they moved on to building comfortable homes that have gardens, backyards, and patios. Cities and skyscrapers sprang up around the world. Societies became modernized. As their technology flourished, in their religions, arts, philosophy, songs, poetry, myths, prayers, and literature, men, women, and children continued to introspect about God and about the *meanings* and *truths* of their lives.

In this 3rd millennium, people now dine on hundreds of gourmet choices for foods and drinks. They can access information and entertainment wherever they may be, and instantly send personal, financial, political and military communications to any other part of the world through the internet and intelligent phones, which humans themselves invented. Even toddlers can now push buttons to open to cartoons, movies, and to stockpiles of information about almost everything on earth! People can have zoom conferences and face to face meetings with any one person or with many; at any time, in any place in the world.

Incredibly, we, the descendants of those grunting human cave dwellers from 200,000 years ago who had no spoken or written language yet, now exist as 240 countries who globally speak and write about 7,000 different languages!

Since the 17th and 18th centuries however, the new breed of humans called *intellectuals* who rose to prominence and seats of power, **belittled** religions, morality, cultural traditions, invisible realities, and even God! As a result, human behaviors regressed, and our human condition deteriorated.

Chapter 2
HURTFUL TEACHINGS of the INTELLECTUALS

The three massive intellectual movements that tampered with the minds of people, cut off the flow of spiritual nurturance to humankind, and caused the human condition to deteriorate were:

I. Modernism and humanism;
II. Sigmund Freud's unproven sexual and other theories; and
III. Existentialism.

I. MODERNISM AND HUMANISM

During the Middle Ages in Europe which lasted from about 500 to 1500 A.D., kings and queens ruled the lands. The serfs provided the needed labor. The Catholic Church was in ascendance and almost everyone was focused on God and religion.

Toward the end of the Middle Ages, a great interest in the study of the classical literature and culture of the Greeks and Romans developed across Europe. This massive intellectual and cultural **shift** in Europe's interest from religion and the outside world, to their inner humanhood, personal dreams, powers, and potentials became known as *Humanism*.

Humanism was one of the factors that gave rise to the *Renaissance*, the movement from 1400 to 1600 characterized by an emphasis on human interests, rather than on the natural world or the heavenly. The Renaissance became the transition between the Middle Ages and Modernism.

Modernism began about 1500 and extends to the present day.

Modernism and humanism brought goodness to our world. These movements awakened, disciplined, taught the masses to think, discover, and reason for oneself; and helped develop our world into what it is today.

In the 17th and 18th centuries however, the intellectuals in the Age of Reason and Age of Enlightenment became over-confident about the powers of their minds and they initiated a movement to *attain human perfectibility **apart from God.***

Voltaire (1694 -1778), the leader of the French thinkers of the Enlightenment called *philosophes,* said: "*We must have the courage to go a few steps further.*"[26]

One *philosophe* gave warning about ...

> "*a great revolution coming in both religion and government.*" It will be an age, he said, that will "*get rid of all revelation and mystery.*" ... Still another wrote, "*I would sacrifice my life if I could annihilate forever the notion of God.*" [27]

---

[26] Ibid. Giles, Anthony E., *People of God: The History of Catholic Christianity* (Ohio: Franciscan Media, 2000), 149.

[27] Ibid. (Bold were added.)

These intellectuals then

> ...proclaimed the death of the Christian God. <u>The universe,</u> they proclaimed, <u>runs according to mechanical laws</u> that can be ascertained by scientific study. Science, not religion, leads humanity to the truth. Formerly Christian Europe eagerly heeded the new gospel of this Age of Enlightenment.[28]

Those teachings of the *philosophes* won great followings and spread broadly over the earth.

As a teen-ager growing up in the Philippines in the 1950's, I was among those who enthused and applauded as humanism, modernism and the sciences taught people the powers of reason, the independence of the mind, and the freedom to be all that one's heart desires! With most of the populace, I presupposed that the newly found powers of the mind and the tools of science *could* take the place and *will do better* than the legacies from the olden times.

When humanism and modernism *allowed* women, men and children to turn away *from* respect towards the elderly, *from* responsibilities towards others, *from* the moral dictates of right versus wrong, and *from* reverence for the divine – the masses, myself included, did not think there was anything dangerous about it. Most of us thought these shifts in behaviors were merely the passing away of the old and the take-over of modernism.

We the populace did not realize until too late, that when the new breed of humans who called themselves the **intellectuals**, tampered with the minds of us, the masses, that our acts of turning our backs to our God, religion, cultural

---

[28] Ibid., 147. (Underlines were added for emphasis.)

traditions, and moral guidelines, would be **like scissors that cut off the flow of the spirit** to our hearts, bodies, and minds!

Just as without sunlight, the earth had darkened and all its vegetation and living creatures perished; in that same way, without the guidance and nurture of the *spirit* for the past 400 years, humanity became like a *tree cut off from its roots*. The moods, worldviews, and thought processes of humans darkened. The human condition deteriorated. And the behaviors of people became erratic, immoral, weird, violent, destructive, cowardly, sinister, and meaningless.

1. The 1ˢᵗ layer that dried up in people, was their *élan*; their enthusiasm, courage, hopefulness, love of life, capacity to endure, and other spiritual capacities. It is sad to see, even among the healthy, normal, and working populations, the increasing number of people around us who lost hope and who gave up completely.

Some may remember the dairy farmer in New York who, in 2010, when the U.S. economy continued to downturn, shot and killed 51 of his milking cows, then himself. A reader named AnnMarie responded thus:

> *When I read this story... I wished I knew this man. Yes, my own life is busy, but I could have gone down even a couple of times a week... learned how a dairy farm like his worked, milked a few dozen cows.... The saddest part was that he may have thought that no one cared anymore. I did.* [29]

---

[29] Comment by a reader, AnnMarie, to *"NY Dairy Farmer kills his cows, then himself,"* by Teri Conroy. http://blog.timesunion.com/farmlife, 1/23/2010.

Two years earlier, in November 2008, a select audience of men and women paid to watch a Florida male teen-ager live-stream his suicide on the internet. This audience watched *until he died!* The coldness of heart of that internet audience was an unnerving new low for humans.[30]

Last year, in June 2020, when Siya Kakkar, a popular 16-yo female TikTok celebrity committed suicide, a reader named Greg wrote,

> *There is something wrong with us. We seek fake empty platforms… for fake empty fame and praise… and claim our lives are well and thriving. Then we take our lives because of what?* **None of it was real**. *It had no substance…. There **was a time** when people fought for themselves and others **to live**. Today, our youth fight to die. Figure that one out.*[31]

Worldwide, there is now on average, *"one death* [by suicide] ***every 20 seconds*** *and one attempt every 1-2 seconds."*[32]

2. The 2nd layer that went out of whack in people, was their *minds*. The causes of the disorders of the mind are still unknown but mental illnesses are now a worldwide concern.

---

[30] *"Florida Teen Live-Streams His Suicide Online,"* by Emily Freedman, *http:abcnews.go.com /Technology,* Nov 21, 2008.
[31] *http://www.yahoo.com/news/remembering-16-old-siya-kakkar-083148287.html,6/26/2020.* (Bold was added.)
[32] Jose Bertolote and Alexandra Fleischmann, "*Suicide and psychiatric diagnosis: a worldwide perspective*", https://www.ncbi.nim.nih.gov/PMC1489848/#:- text=In the year 2020%2C approximately, attempt 1-2 seconds. (Bold were added)

In the U.S. nowadays, whether one is in one's home, neighborhood, classroom, on the streets, malls, airplanes, laundry places, and almost anywhere you go, at any time of day or night; there are unmistakable telltale signs, too widespread to ignore, that people's moods, worldviews, thought processes, and behaviors are out of kilter.

This book assigns the **cause** of the deterioration in our human condition, values, behaviors, and thought processes on **rationalism**; the doctrine which **belittles** the invisible, spiritual, reality, religion, and God, and teaches people that in determining their opinions, course of action, or solutions to problems, they should rely **only** *upon reason.*

> In *philosophy*, people are to consider *reason* to be the true source of knowledge, not the senses.

> In *theology*, people are to reject revelation and the supernatural, and make *reason* the sole source of knowledge.

> In *psychology*, rationalism popularized the use of **"white lies;"** the devising of superficially rational or plausible explanations for one's acts, beliefs, desires, etc., *whether or not* people are aware that these are *not* their real motives.

The grim and gruesome outcome of *rationalism* is a new, violent, troubling, and dismaying psychic disorder, where a child, man, or woman *suddenly mutates* from the normal person that they have been, kills their loved ones and/or themselves, and then provides an *odd, bizarre,* and *naive rationalization* or "white lie," as an excuse for the killings they have committed.

Here are some examples:
a) In 1918, a grandson shot and killed his grandfather and then explained, *"I was only obeying my grandmother"* so that he and his grandmother can spend the grandfather's money.

b) In 2008, a father and his wife in California lost both their jobs at a hospital, after a dispute with an administrator. The father killed his wife, their five children, and then himself. *"The police... found the bodies of the three daughters next to the father.... The boys were with their mother in a back bedroom...."* A suicide note written by both parents explained that *"they did not want their children in foster homes."* [33]

c) In November 2019, a previously normal 16-year-old male high school student, shot 6 of his classmates and then himself, *on his birthday*. We can only wonder what superficial *rationale* was in his mind.

This violent and sad disorder seems to afflict women, children, and men who settle everything **_only_** through use of their intellect and reason; those who live out their existence _not_ in real life but "inside" their imagination and fantasies.

3.. The 3rd and deepest layer in people that warped, is our _human nature_ itself. Our human nature is no longer normal, natural, moral, or sturdy. In unforeseen and disheartening ways, sectors of our lovely, well-educated, and intelligent people have warped into *deviant* and *fiendish beings*.

ONE deviant and fiendish warping of our human nature is **_abortion_** - the voluntary, willful, heartless, and cruel killing of babies by their mothers, while in their wombs.

---

[33] From *"Man Kills his Wife and 5 Children,"* http:www.nytimes.com /2009/01/28.

Among lower forms of animals, mothers will give up their own lives to protect the babies in their wombs or nests.

But among humans, in the year 2008 alone, 44 million human mothers, through the services of Planned Parenthood and their abortion clinics and hospitals, killed their innocent and helpless babies while inside their wombs: 6 million of those abortions were in developed countries and 38 million in the developing countries.[34]

Some mothers do abortion to get rid of unwanted pregnancies. Some countries of the world do abortion to control population growth. An unknown percentage of these babies are dismembered at the abortion hospitals and clinics, and their body parts are sold for cloning experimentations, stem cell studies, and other medical researches.

In the U.S., abortion is supported by the Democrat & Progressive Party and by some sectors of the Catholic, Christian, and liberal religions.

The Republican Party and most Catholic, Christian, and conservative religions want to end this killing of innocent babies.

ANOTHER deviant and fiendish warping of our human nature is the **killings in the name of a religion and their god**, of innocent men, women, and children.

On August 20, 2014, an entire tribe of warped humans showed its face and shocked the world!

On a desert plain in the Middle East, one member of this deviant tribe of humans, a Muslim jihadist who grew up

---

[34] *"In 2008, six million abortions were performed in developed countries and 38 million in developing countries...," http://www.guttmacher.org/media/presskits/abortion-WW/statsand facts.html*, 9/10/2015.

and was educated in London, beheaded an innocent, unarmed and kneeling American journalist dressed in orange, whose hands were tied behind his back. This coldblooded killing, was carefully staged, filmed, and shown to the whole world, by this faction of Muslims.

A few weeks later, this same male Islamic jihadist beheaded two more innocent men, dressed in orange, their hands tied behind their backs. These killings were also staged, filmed, and shown to the world.

Then these Muslims staged, filmed, and showed to the world the beheadings of 100 more men, dressed in orange, with their hands tied behind their backs, and kneeling.

This tribe of grotesque Muslims remain sane, mentally intelligent, and mechanically functional, but they had lost their *spirituality,* that capacity that makes them human.

II. SIGMUND FREUD'S UNPROVEN SEXUAL AND OTHER THEORIES

Sigmund Freud (1856-1939) pioneered and became the founder of psychoanalysis[35] in the early 1900's. His sexual and other theories changed how we humans think of ourselves, our minds, sex, childhood, drives, religion, God, and other aspects of our humanhood. ***But not for the better.***

After World War I [1914-18], in which his own sons fought for Austria, Freud became disillusioned with human nature.

---

[35] *Psychoanalysis* is a method of analyzing psychic phenomena and treating emotional disorders that emphasizes the importance of the patient's talking freely about oneself while under treatment, especially about childhood experiences and about one's dreams.

Freud wearied of the endless slaughter. He grew appalled at the chauvinism of intellectuals, the callousness of commanders, the stupidity of politicians.[36]

So Freud proposed to single-handedly improve the culture of humanity. He reasoned that if the production of wealth is maximized; the populace kept happy and content by making sure that the distribution of wealth is done fairly; and everyone enjoys the wealth they helped to produce; then the golden age *can be attained.*

But he saw two obstacles to his plan:

The **1ˢᵗ obstacle was human nature** because *"there are present in all men destructive, and therefore anti-social and anti-cultural, trends and that in a great number of people these are strong enough to determine their behaviour in human society."*[37]

Freud anticipated that people will rebel and protest if they are forced to work, forced to share with others, or even forced to be happy *"For masses are lazy and unintelligent; they have no love for instinctual renunciation, ... and the individuals composing them support one another in giving free reign to their indiscipline."* (Freud, Illusion, 8)

Using the laziness and lack of intelligence of the masses as the reasons, Freud proposed that instead of government imposing laws and regulations, which are a form of *"external coercion,"* societies should quietly implant their societal rules and regulations into the minds of little

---

[36] Peter Gay, "Sigmund Freud: A Brief Life," Introduction to Sigmund Freud, *The Future of an Illusion* (New York: W. W. Norton & Company, 1989), xix.

[37] Sigmund Freud, *The Future of an Illusion* (New York: W.W. Norton, 1978), 8.

children, during the early years of grade school education in the schools.

Freud's explanation below was compelling.

> *Every child presents this process of transformation to us; only by that means does it become a moral and sexual being. .... Those in whom it has taken place are turned from being opponents of civilization into being its vehicles. The greater their number is in a cultural unit the more secure is its culture and the more it can dispose with external measures of coercion.* (14)

The **2nd obstacle for Freud was religion** because religious ideas can resist and withstand the societal teachings implanted through the schools and even those implanted through psychoanalytic treatments. Religious beliefs, once internalized in childhood, are *"unassailable."*[38]

Freud thereby set out to diminish the value of religion. In his book, *The Future of an Illusion,* Freud explained that religion was *"born from man's need to make his helplessness tolerable and built up from the material of memories of the helplessness of his own childhood and the childhood of the of the human race."* (60)

Per Freud, there is no need for religion in the modern world because *psychology will replace religion* in treating the fears and helplessness in people.

---

[38] *"Thus by the time the child's intellect awakens, the doctrines of religion have already become unassailable."* Ibid., 60.

> *If this view is right, it is to be supposed that a turning-away from religion is bound to occur with the fatal inevitability of a process of growth ....* (55)

If societies will follow his methodology, Freud forecasted that,

> *New generations, who have been brought up in kindness and taught to have a high opinion of reason, and who have experienced the benefits of civilization at an early age, ... will be ready for its sake to make sacrifices as regards work and instinctual satisfaction that are necessary for its preservation. ... If no culture has so far produced human masses of such quality, it is because no culture has yet devised regulations which will influence men in this way, and in particular from childhood onwards.* (9-10)

By the 1920's, when he published this book, the psychoanalytic movement was flourishing. Freud now popular, had become a household word. When he urged schools to experiment with **irreligious education**, the American physicians who came to Vienna to be Freud's personal "pupils" and later returned to practice in New York and Chicago, convinced the American educators to <u>remove religion</u> from the public grade schools in the U.S. and <u>replace them with sex education</u>, even until the present time.[39]

---

[39] Even after Freud *"... was operated on for a growth in his palate... had cancer... compelled to wear a prosthesis ... [and] was rarely free of discomfort or pain.... ... he continued to analyze patients, many of them American physicians who came to Vienna as his "pupils" and returned to analyze in New York and Chicago....."* Peter Gay, *"Sigmund Freud: A Brief Life"* in <u>The Future of an Illusion</u> (New York: W. W. Norton & Company, 1989), xxi. (Word in parenthesis in this footnote was added for clarity).

In that same book, Freud **invited** those who doubted him to **assess the outcome** of his theories *in the future*, saying-

> ... *my illusions are not, like religious ones, incapable of corrections. They have not the nature of a delusion.*
>
> ***If experience should show***—*not to me, but to others after me, who think as I do – that **we have been mistaken, we will give up our expectations**. Take my attempt for what it is. A psychologist who does not deceive himself about the difficulty of finding one's bearings in this world, makes an endeavor to assess the development of man, through a study of processes of individuals during their development from child to adult. ....*
>
> *These discoveries from individual psychology may be **insufficient**, their application to the human race **unjustified**, and his optimism **unfounded**. I grant you all these uncertainties.*
>
> *But often one cannot refrain from saying what one thinks, and one excuses oneself on the ground that **one is not giving it out for more than it is worth**.*[40]

Now in 2021, 82 years after his death, in response to Freud's above-mentioned invite, this writer presents her **evaluation of the theories**[41] **that Freud gave to humankind**, below:

---

[40] Freud, *The Future of an Illusion*, 67-68. (Bold were added. Freud's paragraph are here printed with a space between paragraph for easier reading)

[41] My eligibility to evaluate the outcome of Freud's theories are based on my 3 years' work as a social worker among foster families in the south

I. Freud's theories in individual psychology about phobia, paranoia, and obsessional neurosis listed below, **are insufficient** because they were only based on **one-case studies**. To be scientifically certified, they should have been corroborated by a few more other studies.

- Little Hans: *"Analysis of a Phobia in a Five-year-old Boy;"*
- Rat Man: *"Notes Upon a Case of Obsessional Neurosis;"*
- Schreber Case: *"Psycho-Analytic Notes on an Autobiographical Account of a Case of Paranoia."*

II. By reason that Freud's discoveries from individual psychology were not scientifically proven and verified as theories; therefore, **Freud was not justified** in applying his personal opinions and hypotheses, including these listed below, as **"cures"** and **"remedies"** for the mental, emotional, and social ills of the human race.

1. His opinion that the nature of the unconscious is sexual.
2. His hypothesis that all dreams are wish-fulfillments.
3. His speculation that religion can be replaced by psychology in calming human fears towards the mysteries of the universe.
4. His opinion that the teaching of religion in grade schools to young children serves no purpose.

---

suburbs of Chicago; 5 years' work as a Senior Psychiatric Therapist in the Psychiatric E/R of a medical center in Jersey City; my M.A. in Pastoral Counseling degree from Loyola University in Chicago, and my 34 years of documented dream and personal developmental experiences in the *spirit*.

5. His opinion that the goal of human life is *pleasure*.
6. His supposition that to be healthy and happy adults, men and women should explore their oral, anal, and other erotic drives from infancy to adulthood.
7. His conjectural id-ego-superego schematic of the mind.

III. **Freud's optimism** that his theories will usher in the golden age for humankind **was unfounded**. Per what we see around us, the outcome of his unproven sexual and other theories:
1. Deranged people's minds, morals, characters, and behaviors.
2. Encouraged excessive promiscuity and uninhibited sexual practices that wrecked marriages, careers, and families, and trampled on morality and the laws of Nature.
3. Stimulated the painful and lifelong gender confusion among adults and children.
4. Fostered the spread of pedophilia.
5. Gave rise to the dirty industries of kidnapping and selling of children and women into sexual enslavement. And,
6. Profaned and mocked the practice of religion; disfigured the unconscious and spiritual realm in humans; and muddled the destiny of the human race.

IV. **In the U.S., Freud's irreligious education experiment has failed**! The two and three generations of children in U.S. public schools who were not taught religion but were taught sex education instead; **did not pick up** good work ethics or the readiness to make sacrifices for the common good, as Freud had speculated.

V. OVER-ALL, Freud gave to humanity unproven and unverified sexual and other theories for far **"more than they were worth."**

TO UNDO FREUD'S GRIEVOUS ERRORS,
the U.S. should immediately:
- end Freud's irreligious experiment in our public grade schools;
- stop the teaching of sexual education before the 5th grade in public grade schools; and,
- bring back the teaching of religion, civic duties, history, myths, and classics to our grade schools,

Removing the over-focus on sex will *reduce* its 200,000 *teenage pregnancies* every year.

Reducing teenage pregnancies will correspondingly *reduce* the hundred thousands of *teen-age abortions* and the many thousands of foster children who grow up without fathers, mothers, and stable homes.

Removing the over-focus on sex will also *tone down* the spiraling and hurting epidemic of *gender confusion.*

Instead of sexual education, *bring religion back* to the classrooms as electives and teach our young children how to pray and revere the realm of the divine. As humankind continues to evolve to their state of completeness,[42] our children will need the capacity to understand their dreams, instincts and feelings. *Prayers* will also sow the seeds of humility and *truthfulness in our children*, which will help

---

[42] The stages of our continuing evolution to our state of completeness, through the action of archetypal dreams and instincts, are described in detail in my Book Two.

them *safely* undergo the stages of evolution into spiritual beings in their older years.

Another simple antidote is for people to *tone down* the sexual hype in their own clothes, thoughts, manners, and behaviors.

Star Parker, a syndicated columnist in the U.S., blamed promiscuity and immorality for AIDS, abortion, and the entire welfare state in the U.S.[43] She pleaded for *sexual energy to be reduced,* so people can regain their moral and mental health, and the U.S. economy can recover.

III. EXISTENTIALISM

Existentialism, a 20th century philosophy, went a step further than the Age of Reason and the Age of Enlightenment: This movement completely scalpeled God from creation and the universe.

It declared that no higher power created our universe.
No Divine Providence is guiding our universe.
Our universe simply exists.
The universe is neither moral nor immoral; neither caring or uncaring.
It is just objectively "there," neutral and *absurd.* [44]

---

[43] "*Parker Blames 'Sexual Promiscuity' for Poverty, Government Spending, All Social Problems,*" submitted by Brian Tashman, 1025/2011. http://www.rightwingwatch.org/content/parker-blames-sexual-promiscuity.

[44] *Absurdism* is the philosophical and literary doctrine that human beings live in essential isolation in a meaningless and irrational world.

Because the existentialist universe does not include God, humans live alone in this indifferent universe. To thrive, humankind must have *the capacity to will to act.*

The existentialist Albert Camus [1913-60], in his writings, additionally painted human existence to be dreary. His book, <u>*The Myth of Sisyphus,*</u> describes that life on earth is like the punished life of Sisyphus in the underworld.[45] It is an endless, meaningless task of pushing a rock up a hill, only to see it roll down, again and again.

But per Camus, humans *can* defy and rebel against our *absurd* universe. In that brief moment after the rock has rolled down and before he rolls it up again, the person can become *conscious* and come to the realization that this task is *"his"* struggle. He has the capacity to will to act on his realization that,

> *His fate belongs to him. His rock is his thing. ... the absurd man, when he contemplates his torment, silences all the idols. ... Thus, convinced of the wholly human origin of all that is human, a blind man...who knows that the night has no end, he is still on the go. The rock is still rolling.*[46]

Camus ends his memorable writing as follows:

> *... One always finds one's burden again. But Sisyphus teaches the higher fidelity that negates the gods and raises rocks. He too concludes that all is well. This universe henceforth without a master seems*

---

[45] In Greek mythology, *Sisyphus* was a crafty, greedy king of Corinth, condemned in Hades to forever roll uphill a huge stone, which always rolled down again.

[46] Albert Camus, <u>*The Myth of Sisyphus and Other Essays*</u>, trans. Justin O'Brien (New York: Vintage International, 1983), 123.

to him neither sterile nor futile. Each atom of that stone, each mineral flake of that night-filled mountain, in itself forms a world. The struggle itself toward the heights is enough to fill a man's heart. One must imagine Sisyphus happy. [Ibid.]

In my early 40's, I found Camus' writings challenging, particularly his urging that humans must have the capacity to will to struggle against all odds. But now in my late-70's, I realize that excessive liberalism, pompous intellectualism, Freud's unproven sexual and other theories, existentialism and other anti-God theories, *dangerously misguided* and *almost ruined civilization* to an irreparable extent.

Without God, without religion, without moral guidelines, without family systems, without good schools, without law and order, without the police… and now making marijuana legally available to many? *What are we thinking*? Many still do not realize that without religion, morality, law and order, cultural guidelines, and God, there can be no human safety, meanings, happiness, wellbeing, and destiny.

But take heart.

Chapter 3 which now follows, describes that our human evolution to a higher state of being, is now happening.

Chapter 3
How does human evolution happen?

In his book, *The Phenomenon of Man,* Pierre Teilhard de Chardin (1881-1955) theorized that in our continuing human evolution, the individual consciousness of men, women, and children are being *consolidated* into one huge global consciousness, which he called the *noosphere*. This noosphere will become planet-like in its size and will circle the earth like the rings of Saturn. This merging of individual consciousness into the *noosphere* will continue until the Omega Point is attained.

> ... by structure, the **noosphere**... represent a whole that is not only closed but also centered.... Accordingly its enormous layers, followed in the right direction, must somewhere ahead become involuted to a point which we might call Omega.[47]

---

[47] Pierre Teilhard de Chardin, *The Phenomenon of Man* (New York: Harper and Row, 1959), 59. (Bold was added).

Aldous Huxley, the author of <u>A Brave New World</u>, who wrote the *Introduction* to Teilhard's book, supported Teilhard's theory about the *noosphere* and Teilhard's assumptions that human evolution will be *cephalic* and *directed* by humans themselves.

> *With his genius for fruitful analogy, he* [Teilhard de Chardin] *points out that the process of evolution on earth is itself now in the process of becoming* **cephalised...** *It remains for our descendants to organize this global* **noosystem** *more adequately, so as to* **enable mankind** *to understand the process of evolution on earth more fully and to* **direct it** *more adequately.*[48]

It was because I read a few of Teilhard's books[49] in 1993, six years after my dream experiences began, that I began to understand and take an interest in human evolution. It was his writings that revealed to me the *similarities* between evolution processes as he saw it, and the bizarre and powerful dream experiences that I was going through.

However, my dream experiences *do not support* Teilhard's theories that people's individual consciousness are consolidating into a planet-sized *noosystem*. Nor his assumptions that our evolution will be more of the same: it will merely increase people's *cephalic* or *mental* intelligence and people will *direct* their own evolution.

---

[48] Aldous Huxley, "Introduction," <u>The Phenomenon of Man</u> (New York: Harper & Row, 1959), 20. (Words in brackets and bold were added for clarity and emphasis.)

[49] Some of Teilhard's other books are: *The Future of Man, The Heart of Matter, Hymn of the Universe, Man's Place in Nature,* and *The Divine Milieu.*

As I experienced it, our continuing evolution is not about becoming stronger, wiser, kinder or being a superhuman. Per my experiences, a special group of dreams and instincts are evolving humankind into **individuals** with powers of the mind and powers of the *spirit*, like the Risen Jesus.

These special dreams and instincts that guide our evolution have already been **discovered**, studied, and documented by the psychoanalyst Carl G. Jung. His brief biography, works, and theories are described in Part III of this book.

Jung's theories and his Individuation Paradigm are described in great detail, alongside my dream experiences and related real-life experiences, in my Book Two.

The rest of this chapter will now briefly narrate how my own evolutionary journey began and give samples of the general types of extra-sensory experiences that I underwent. A few question-and-answer descriptions of our human evolution are also included.

Let me start my narration by qualifying that all my life, I had always assumed that God lives up *there* in heaven and we humans exist down *here,* on earth; and the *there* and the *here* do not ever meet until *after* we die. While we live, God watches over us, protects us, and is *near* to us – but from up *there*.

Never in my wildest imagination did I ever think it possible that God, can actually be "*here,*" where we *are*.

That all changed in the spring of 1987, when the *spirit* actually wrapped itself around me and I felt the *nearness* of God, while I was walking on our walkway.

Two days before that unusual event happened, a man from the sheriff's office came to our door and served me a notice for our eviction from our townhouse. This eviction notice was a follow-up to an earlier letter from the mortgage lender which had informed me that after 4 months of non-payment, they had foreclosed on our townhouse.

I was 45 years old then and a working single mother of 3 sons and a daughter in their early teens. We had been in the U.S. for some years but were still learning how to cope with the ways of the new country. *Where will my 4 children and I move to?* I thought to myself and didn't have an answer.

That Thursday morning when I walked to my car to drive to work, had seemed like other mornings. I sat in the driver's seat and inserted the key in the keyhole when out of the blue, without any warning, all my energies were drained from my body! I suddenly felt so utterly, utterly exhausted that I could not even lift my arm to turn the key to start the car!

For about 3 or 4 minutes, I sat motionless and rigid, as though frozen; my right-hand limp on my lap. I could move my eyes but not my head or body. All I could do was stare at a small, light brown butterfly that had alighted on my windshield at eye level. In my mother's religious traditions, a brown butterfly is believed to be the presence of a dear family member or friend who has passed away. I felt consoled, thinking my late father was with me.

When I could move again, I slowly walked back to our townhouse to call in sick. My exhausted body felt so heavy. Halfway to our townhouse, with my head down, I was surprised to see a bunch of red and pink flowers strewn on our walkway. *An animal must have brought them there because they were not there when I walked out.* Those flowers[50] grow abundantly in the Philippines but I had never seen them here in the U.S.

---

[50] In 2007, 20 years since my experiences began, I saw those same flowers on our walkway in a garden center. That's when I learned that in

Feebly, so I don't step on them, I lifted my left foot a bare few inches above the stems of flowers in front of me. At that moment, when my left foot was in the air above the flowers, a soothing flow of peace and calm buoyed my entire body with such enthusiasm and joy that ***Instantly I knew… without any doubt!*** (even before my left foot touched ground again), ***that things were going to be all right!***

As I walked on, that feeling of peace walked with me. Every step I took washed more and more of my tiredness away. By the time I opened the door to our townhouse, I was so energized that I went in, got me a cup of coffee and 2 pieces of bread, my bank statements, a calculator, my boxes of checkbooks, notepads, and worked non-stop for about 10 hours, tabulating all my mortgage payment checks for the past 5 years against the lender's statements, my bank statements, and postal return slips.

To my great surprise and dismay, around 7 p.m. that evening when I finished, I discovered that 3 of my payment checks which the lender received and cashed, were <u>*not* credited to my account!</u> A postal return receipt showed that the lender also received my 4th payment check but they *did not cash it.*

Next day, as soon as my bank verified my findings, I called my mortgage lender and faxed them copies of my documents and findings. They asked no questions and gave no explanation or apology, but the foreclosure and eviction processes against our townhouse were immediately stopped!

Years later, I understood that because a mortgage lender can foreclose on a property after 4 months of non-payment, my mortgage lender tried to *defraud* us by not

---

the U.S., it is called *balsam*. I looked up the word in the dictionary and learned that balsams are healing, soothing, and medicinal plants.

crediting 3 of my payment checks into my account and by not cashing my 4th payment check. They made it appear that I was in payment default for 4 months and therefore they had ground to foreclose on our townhouse and evict us. The lender would have also cheated us of our 5-year equity in the townhouse!

So relieved that our townhouse was suddenly saved from foreclosure, it didn't even occur to me to take legal action against the lender. And I did not tell my children about the strewn flowers on our walkway because I did not know what that was about.

But for years, I was dumbfounded. I asked myself over and over: *Did God really come to our neighborhood? How did God know about those 4 checks? Why did He help us and not others more worthy or more in need of help? Did He strew those flowers on our walkway? Is God asking me to do something for Him?*

I kept these questions in my heart. Privately, I named our small miracle *an event of grace*.

A few months later, I received 8 deeply religious and mystical dreams that came one behind the other, from 1987 to 1993.

In my past life, I rarely dreamt. In my past 45 years, I might have had 5 or 6 dreams that I recalled when I woke up. So, when those 8 deeply religious dreams were followed by spurts and floods of more perplexing and at times overwhelming dreams and other unusual phenomena, I didn't know how to respond to those happenings.

In the first 15 to 20 years of my dream experiences, images appeared in my consciousness while I slept and at times, even while I was awake. Those strange phenomena and hard-to-explain dreams were a constant surprise!

A visual would pop up in my consciousness while I was sitting in the living room sofa and briefly closed my eyes. Sometimes it happened while I was doing the dishes; closing my eyes to sleep; or waking up from sleep.

Like the proverbial frog in the bottom of a dark well, I had no clue what these uncanny phenomena were about or what was expected of me. Streams of pictorials appeared in my consciousness as one puzzling riddle after another. I didn't know where to begin.

Deep in my heart however, because I was still awed and will always be grateful for the episode of the strewn flowers that saved our townhouse, I felt assured that these bizarre, mysterious and upheaving experiences were happening for a reason. Thus, from the start, I documented all these experiences, partly on impulse and partly out of curiosity. I sketched and described them briefly, including the dates and times I received them and my impressions about them. Those notes and sketches written on whatever paper I could find, later helped me organize and sort out my inner experiences into this book.

My notes also served as testimonies to myself that these strange phenomena *really* did happen!

Some details in my notes I couldn't understand at all, but most of my notes were helpful. A few of my observations served as dots that after some years, connected on their own to reveal new meanings about myself, our human condition, and arranged themselves into clues and patterns that explained *how our dreams relate to the prophecies* since the ancient times.

Thankfully, in my case, after about twelve to fifteen years of being like the frog at the bottom of a dark well, the dreams and unusual inner experiences that flooded my consciousness *slowed down*.[51]

Bit by bit and year by year, I felt a growing inner newness in me. The upheaving experiences that intruded into my sleeping and waking hours began to *deepen* my thought processes, beliefs, worldviews, and behaviors. I began to feel rooted in the *spirit,* felt grounded, and was no longer just chaff in the wind. I began to have convictions, meanings, and the quiet capacity to stand up for what is right versus wrong.

In addition to dreams, people going through their 2nd birthing in the *spirit* will also receive these other forms of extra-sensory experiences:

♦ **VISUALS** - A *visual* is a brief dreamlike episode received while the person is awake. While doing daily activities or meditating, the person could nonchalantly close his or her eyes briefly, and without warning, these *visuals* will play out on that inner backside of our forehead where our dreams also appear.

I warn the readers that *visuals,* especially the earlier ones, <u>are</u> discombobulating! I received about 5 of these frightening and unnerving visuals early on in the first 4 to 5 years of my experiences. My heart would stop when they came, because my early visuals showed a figure of myself tossed about in a deep and turbulent river! But thankfully,

---

[51] Some long-term studies of schizophrenia that I've read, suggest that the dysfunctional and psychotic symptoms in schizophrenia will tone down and normalize around the 12th to the 15th years. My own view is that many of the neuroses, psychoses, and even cases of dementia and Alzheimer's that people suffer from, are stages of our continuing evolution that have gone awry or are not yet fully understood.

there was always a large black and flat **rock** in the river, on which the figure of myself *always safely landed.*

No matter how disconcerted I was by a visual or dream, I would grab the first piece of paper or notebook, describe and document what the visual or dream showed so I could read my notes and think about them later. I also prayed a lot, and at the suggestion of a parish priest who said to me, *"There is grace in receiving communion,"* I also began attending daily Mass before going to work. (I'm Filipina and a Roman Catholic.) In uncanny and soothing ways, the Psalms read during Mass were usually related to my visuals.

Verses like, *"God is my **rock** and my salvation"* were very comforting. That I heard these verses during Mass gave me assurance that God knew about my discombobulating visuals, and therefore, I should trust that there is a reason for why these phenomena were happening to me.

The grace and guidance of the daily Masses, my later graduate courses in theology and psychology at Loyola in Chicago, and my readings seemed to guide me to make a serious effort to be <u>*humble*</u> and <u>*truthful*</u> *even in the littlest things*. Thereupon, I stopped using make-up, stopped wearing high heels, and dressed simply in an effort to have the <u>*humility to accept myself as I truly am.*</u> After some years, as I made some progress in my inner growth, the contents and pictorials of my *visuals*, also changed!

Eight years after my dream experiences began, in 1995, I received a visual in which the turbulent and raging river in my earlier visuals that I so dreaded, was replaced with a calm and peaceful lake! In this recent visual, the figure of myself was no longer tossed about in the raging waters but I was myself as a round-faced plump and well-behaved little girl of six or seven, *safely* sitting on a flat boat with oars, above a clear and peaceful lake, with a kindly man in his 50's. I was surprised and relieved beyond words!

Wordless feeling-tones "spoke" to my consciousness, saying,

> Look as deeply as you can into the waters and do not be afraid. For when you reach out with your left hand or right hand, you will touch land, as in a bathtub.

With my eyes still closed, in my consciousness as the 53-yr-old dreamer now on the boat. I mentally leaned forward from the boat and looked down into the lake. Because the water was still and so clear, I could see that the lake was several *miles* deep. I saw no objects; only clear water. I pulled myself back, slightly repositioned my body, then leaned forward to look down into the waters more deeply, but on this 2nd look, I could only see as far as the equivalent depth of a 2 or 3 story building. Then I began to feel dizzy and the visual ended.

When I thought about it afterwards, I took that visual to mean that I am to learn and understand as much as I can. I have always been an avid reader, but I doubled that effort.

In the years that followed, I read, reread, and reread a few thousand books and I still continue to read all kinds of books. I also took thousands of hours of very slow walks around the streets of the neighborhoods we lived in, mulled about this and that, thought things through, and looked, and listened, and still do. In our Skokie townhouse, when I used to garden in our front yard, the husband of our next-door neighbor looked at me quizzically once or twice and asked, "*Why do you walk so slowly?*" I smiled and said that I was "*mulling about some concepts*."

In those early years when I was like the frog in a dark well, even as I was coping with the unknowables of my visuals, I was also concurrently living through the mandates, wonders, and unknowable of my 1st, 2nd, 3rd, and other dreams! This is why people who are going through their 2nd birthing in the *spirit* should diary their dreams and other experiences, and why prayers and private time for oneself are necessary. Because the person will have so many inscrutable and mystical strangeness to *concurrently* cope with. But no matter how difficult the going is, **do not ever *lie* to the *spirit*** and **do not take shortcuts**. In the Telos, *lies, arrogance,* and *indifference* will have immediate, hurtful, and dangerous repercussions. Without truthfulness, sincerity of heart, and humility, your inner journey *can* quickly deteriorate into delusions, phobias, depression, and other emotional and mental disorders, or other mishaps.

My later visuals, which are described in my Book Two, showed that over the years, I did cross over to the other side of the waters on that boat. My last visual in 1998, which I received while sitting beside my unknowing sister Marge, on an airplane, returning back to the U.S. after our visit to the Philippines for Mama's 1st death anniversary, showed a figure of me near the top of a mountain. That was consoling because the mountain is a religious symbol for the nearness of God.

♦ **TRANCE** – I received a *trance* only once. It happened in 1998, 11 years after my dream experiences began. In a *trance,* the person is awake, conscious, and one's eyes remain open. But *voluntary* movement *is briefly lost.* The person cannot move, as though he or she is in hypnosis, daze, stupor or stunned condition.

While in the Philippines for Mama's 1st death anniversary, we had stayed in the home of my brother Farley and his wife Raquel. On one noon time, I was walking in their orchid garden when I happened to look up and fell into a *trance*. Frozen and immobile for about a minute or two, with my head turned to my left, my body slightly turned leftward and looking up, I watched as *waves of thoughts* traveled in straight lines from the sun to the top of my head. Because my head was tilted upwards, I could see the *waves* and marveled at how, when they touched my head, they gently explained to me why I received God's frightening *reprimand* in my 3rd dream in 1988, ten years earlier.

In those early years of my experiences, after I began attending daily Mass, I also volunteered to help with the successful Renew Program in that parish. I did good work but felt uncomfortable doing parish work, So, before I slept one night, I asked God in prayer if I could end my parish volunteer work. I explained to God in that prayer that I would continue to do volunteer work, but would it all right if I did it in a *secular* setting?
I was awakened that night by a *reprimand* from God in my 3rd dream that was so frightening, my body would tremble and shake in fear whenever I thought about it. My state of fear and trembling lasted for months! I protested to God in another prayer and begged Him to stop sending me these dreams, because I don't understand what these experiences are about, and I couldn't handle them anymore! To my great surprise, the dreams did stop for 3 years and 3 months. Then, they came back again but my later dreams were in *gentler* forms.

This *trance* which I received 10 years later, in 1998, was God's answer to my protest in 1988, ten years earlier!

I realized then that God did not forget my protest but waited some years, so that He could explain to me, in a way that I could understand why He sent me that frightening *reprimand* in my 3rd dream.

I felt humbled and awed that God took that bother for someone as insignificant as myself, in a personal and caring way. *It must be true that God knows and cares for us so completely, He has counted the number of hairs on our head.*[52]

♦ **VISIONS** - In early 1992, a few months before I was terminated at work, I received two visions at the exact same part in two consecutive morning Masses I attended. I received one vision for each day.

A *vision* is similar to a visual in that the person is awake and one's eyes are briefly closed. What sets a vision apart is its deeply *religious* content. A *vision* may reveal a *religious prophecy,* or the person may see *an image* of a divine being, as I did.

On those two mornings in a Chapel during Mass, with my eyes closed and while I was standing with the congregation during the early part of the Mass, I briefly closed my eyes and saw visions of the Crucified Christ and of the Risen Christ.

Jung mentioned somewhere in his writings that when a person "sees" an image or vision of a divine being, the deity is *not actually* present. The vision is showing a specific *characteristic* or *trait* of the deity as embodied in that image, that applies to the person.

But when I received my visions 29 years ago, I could not grasp any clues for why I received them.

---

[52] *"Are not five sparrows sold for two farthings, and not one of them is forgotten by God? Indeed, the very hairs of your head are all numbered. Don't be afraid; you are worth more than many sparrows."* Luke 12:7.

Every few years, those visions would come to mind, and I wondered some more about why I received them.

Now in 2021, I am beginning to sense the *weight of the responsibility* that those 2 visions have placed on my shoulders.

Even though I still do not fully understand what God is asking me to do, because of the recent onslaughts of the coronavirus, the lawlessness and other forms of social, political, and religious upheavals in the U.S. and other parts of the world, I am fearful about the seriousness and weight of my unknown task. I worry that I may *not* be able to cope with this load allotted to me.

As Carl Jung is quoted saying in chapter 6 of this book, *"The images of the unconscious place a great responsibility upon a man."* And upon a woman.

♦ **A SIGN FROM GOD** – A *sign from God* is a dream or visual sent *"from above"* to answer a question that was asked in a prayer, as to whether or not God wants the person to undertake a certain action or decision.

One night in the early fall of 1993, a few weeks after I began my studies at Loyola in Chicago, it occurred to me that perhaps God wants me to write a book about my dream experiences.

So, I prayed to God that if He wanted me to write a book about my unusual experiences, to please send me the *title of a book* as confirmation.

Then I lay me down to sleep.

As I was still closing my eyes, and even while I was still awake, I dreamt of a desk daily calendar.

On its page were written,
   "Peace, Prosperity, and Today,"
with the words written one below the other.

I took these words to be a sign from God, confirming what my task is.

These 4 words are now the title of the series of three books that I am in the process of writing.

This 1ˢᵗ *sign from God* in 1993 told me, the **title** for the book or books that I am to write.

Then, in 2003, 10 years later, I received a 2ⁿᵈ *sign from God* in a visual, which told me the **subject matter** that I am to write about. The visual showed a small slip of yellow pad paper and on it was a handwritten sentence that said,

   "You must make it
      and write about the **Tree of Life**.*"*

Since 2003, for 16 years, I wrote over a hundred versions of this book, but none of it was it. I'd come to a point where I couldn't continue, and I'd stop. Then start on another draft after some months.

Only in March of this year, when on the 1st paragraph of the 1st page of this book, I used a quote from Genesis about the *Tree of Life* in God's garden in Eden, did this book move on to publication.

In this last portion of this chapter, I include some questions that readers might ask, about our continuing evolution:

♦ ***During the stages of one's evolution**, can people manipulate their dreams and instincts so that they can evolve any way they want to?*

The answer is No. All living things have natural boundaries of *time*, *space*, and *death* that they cannot break out of. Those who transgress against the boundaries of their nature or disobey the cosmic laws will undergo illnesses, regressions, transmogrifications, or annihilation.

This forbiddance is necessary because a *change* in an element or creature, no matter how insignificant and simple it may be, must *not* interfere or infringe on the freedom, configuration and destiny of each and all the myriads of other creatures and elements in Creation.

Only God can create a *new* structure, power, function, element, or living thing that did *not* previously exist in creation, since only God the Creator can ensure that whatever *changes* are made will *not* infringe on the *freedom* and *uniqueness* of each and all elements and creatures in creation.

♦ **Are there ways to know** <u>when</u> and <u>how</u> these stages of evolution will happen?

Yes, to some extent.

As to *when*: Our 2nd birthing in the *spirit* generally begins around midlife and continues to the end of one's lifetime. The mid-lifers and senior people are the ones on the front lines of the final stages of our evolution.

Although not all men and women going through mid-life will be "taken," it is good caution for them to stay away from marijuana and other pollutants that can hinder or skew their chances for a safe 2nd birthing in the *spirit*.

Also know that evolution to one's state of wholeness is not completed within anyone's lifetime. It seems to be carried forward along the lineage of every person, from generation to generation, until the state of wholeness is attained for that lineage; this may take thousands of generations more.

As to *how*: The *spirit* "takes" men, women, and possibly children at random and in unknowable times and places.

> *That night two people will be asleep in one bed; one will be taken, the other left. Two women will be grinding flour together in the mill; one will be taken, the other left. (Lk 17: 34-35)*

Those "taken" will live in *two different realms* of reality during the rest of their lifetime. They continue to live and function in the real world as best they can, and concurrently, in their inner and subjective world, they are wrapped inside a chrysalis, so to speak, and they undergo uncanny, mystical life experiences and challenges under the guidance of a special group of dreams and impulses.

Because of the dual world that they live in, those men, women, and children going through stages of evolution will tend to be withdrawn; are more religious; and may manifest hard-to-explain behaviors and outlooks in life. At the end of their lifetime, their progress or lack of progress are probably added or subtracted from the cumulative progress of their lineage.

Those who undergo their 2nd birthing should carefully and truthfully document and *share* their evolutionary experiences, to make it easier for those in the future to undergo their inner journeys safely.

♦ **On a scale of 0 to 10,** wit*h 10 as highest, what are the chances that a person will complete his or her portion of evolutionary journey safely?*

The chances are slim.

What makes these journeys difficult is that the symbols in these dreams are tied to the prophecies and to our ancient past which we moderns know little about.

Therefore, read books about myths, religions, ancient beliefs and rituals, and get into the habit of listening and getting to know your inner world. You will need the guidance of religions, classics, folklores, and cultural and moral legacies from the ancient past in order to correctly interpret the symbols, plots, and other elements of your dreams.

Those who have strong familiarity with their religion, cultural and moral traditions, literature, legacies, and their inner worlds, may have a chance of 3 to 6, because they will have a better chance of interpreting the riddles, moral guidelines, and prophetic guidelines of their dreams.

It will be harder for those who have no religion and who are out of touch with their traditions and inner world. Their chances may be between 0 and 4 because their tendency may be to dismiss or be indifferent to their dreams. Or they may interpret the mystical and religious symbols and plots of their dreams in a *mental* or *literal* way, which almost always leads to mishaps and perils.

Expect your evolutionary journeys to be lonely climbs because you, the person in journey, will not know what you are going through and will not have the words to explain yourself to families, friends, and others. They and you as well, will have no clue what, why, and where you are going. It helped me greatly to document my experiences, so I had something concrete to lean on and ponder about.

It also helps to read a lot and think deeply. Have confidence in yourself and do not be afraid.

The most helpful factors are truthfulness, humility, a sincere heart, trust, and prayer. In my journey, these were the factors that saved me from peril. These factors are really what make or break one's journey.

♦ **Is cloning** *a form of continuing evolution?*

No. A clone is a humanlike organism derived through a process similar to grafting or budding in plants. A clone is *not* a true human being. It is only a "copy" of a person *up to that point* in time of that individual's existence. It will have a living brain and mind, but its thoughts, values, worldviews and behaviors will probably be reruns of the thoughts, values, worldviews and behaviors of the individual that it was grafted or cloned from.

The clone, which is born in a test tube, is *not* God's creation. It will not possess a realm of the *spirit*; will not experience true dreams; cannot reproduce; and cannot evolve to a higher state of being.

In contrast, a true human being is a man or woman born from a mother's womb; it is flesh born out of flesh.

Only a true human being will undergo a 2nd birthing in the *spirit* and see and enter the kingdom of God on earth while still living.

◆ **What dangers** *are encountered?*

These are some dangers to avoid during one's evolutionary journey:

1) ***Do not <u>arrogant</u> and <u>indifferent</u>*** to your dreams and other manifestations of your unconscious. *Arrogance* can lead to delusions of grandeur. *Indifference* to and repressions of these spiritual communications and guidance from the Telos can lead to anxiety, tics, restlessness, paranoia, and other forms of neurosis.

2) ***Do not <u>underestimate</u>* your dreams and other extra-sensory experiences,** even when they appear primitive, cartoonish or unimportant. These dreams and instincts are connected to cosmic laws and prophecies and have cosmic authority and tremendous powers.

3) **Do <u>not</u> submit yourself <u>completely</u>** to the powers and allure of these dreams and inner experiences. Keep one foot in your inner world and the other foot in real life, so as to keep your balance and sanity. Trust yourself and your common sense. Allowing yourself to be lured and overwhelmed by your dreams and visuals, can lead to

delusions of grandeurs, schizophrenia, and other forms of psychosis.[53]

♦ Is a 2nd birthing in the *spirit* worth the hardships that come with it?

Before my experiences in the spirit, I was relatively happy, popular and successful. But I could not find lasting peace. Even when I was good, kind, felt "at home" and in harmony with other people; inside myself, something was still missing. My inner and outer selves were not the same person.

I now realize that I felt "unfinished" because I did not yet know about the *realm of the spirit*. I only saw visible reality through my senses, brain and mind and had mistakenly concluded that the physical world is *all* of reality! That there is *nothing more*.

In that existence of halfness, I was like chaff. Tugged and pulled by forces of benevolence and aggression that were beyond my control. I felt helpless. No matter how hard I tried, existence seemed fickle and offered no peace or lasting joy.

But everything changed after I was *"taken"* and re-born in the *spirit*. In this period of my life now, I have a degree of peace that I did not think was possible for me to have in this life. I am not holier, nor happier, nor am I on a higher state of being.

The best way I can explain it, is that I am now "grounded" or "seeded" like wheat. My feeling at this time

---

[53] *Psychosis* is a mental disorder, severe in character, often involving a disorganization of the total personality.

of my life is, I know *"where"* I am and *"who"* I am. This sense of identity and knowing the purpose of my life are more than I ever hoped to find.

Part II which follows will describe more characteristics of the Telos.

Part II
Characteristics of the Telos or *spirit*

*We teach what scripture
 calls the things
  that no eyes have seen
  and no ear has heard,
     all that God has prepared,
     for those who love Him.*
          I Cor. 2: 9

Chapter 4
PSYCHIC ENERGIES and INVISIBLE PARTICLES THAT ARE <u>NOT</u> *SPIRIT*

How can we distinguish the Telos from psychic energies and quantum particles that are *matter*?

The litmus test is, if the invisible phenomenon, particle, force, or power *can* be captured, studied, and manipulated by human will, gadgets and techniques, then it is matter; not *spirit*.

We know for instance, that the Higgs boson or so-called "God particle," neutrinos,[54] and energies including sound, gravity, magnetism, and electricity, which *can* be captured and manipulated by human gadgets, are <u>*not*</u> *spirit*.

This chapter will differentiate the Telos from the invisible psychic energies known as *kundalini, chakras, aura,* and *chi,* and from *quantum particles*.

---

[54] The *neutrino* is a neutral particle smaller than a neutron, having a mass approaching zero.

1. KUNDALINI

Per Hindu writings,

> *In human beings the surplus of energy that is not being used to maintain the functioning of the organism is also symbolically described as a coiled or resting serpent.*
> *This potential energy is said to rest at the base of the spinal cord....*
> *The potential energy is called **kundalini**. Kundalini is the static support of the entire body and all its pranic or energic forces.*[55]

By using a technique like yoga and in a process that will take many years to complete, a person can "awaken" this resting *kundalini* and guide it to unwind and slowly rise to the crown of one's head.

As the *kundalini* rises, it is said to feel like heat, electric current, or feelings of pleasure in the spine region.

> *As the kundalini awakens there is a sensation of something moving along the spine.*
> *This has been described as a feeling of frogs jumping, snakes wriggling, or ants creeping in a line from the feet to the head.*[56]

---

[55] Swami Rama, "The Awakening of Kundalini," in *Kundalini, Evolution and Enlightenment*, ed. John White (New York: Anchor Book, 1979), 29. (Bold was added.)

[56] Ibid., 42.

The higher the kundalini rises, the more it endows the yoga practitioner with enlightenment, bliss, and even divinity.

Those extraordinary people called yogis, who are adept and who can guide the *kundalini* to rise towards one's head will receive its powers.

One difference between the *spirit* and the *kundalini* is, that the *kundalini* is matter. When the person is born, its *kundalini* is "sleeping," resting at the base of one's vertebrae and has to be "awakened" using yoga.
The *spirit*, on the other hand, is autonomous and living.

A 2nd difference between *kundalini* and the Telos is the powers of the *kundalini* are available only to those men, women and children who can master yoga.
The Telos, in contrast, is like the sun and the rain that ongoingly sustain, nourish, and nurture *all* elements and creatures.

Thirdly, the Telos is vaster than the *kundalini*. While the *kundalini* resides in one person, the Telos is the womb that contains the universe and everything in it.

Fourthly, the *kundalini* whose nature is matter, will die with the person.
The Telos whose nature is immortal *spirit,* lives forever.

2. CHAKRAS

According to the ancient yogis, the rising of the *kundalini* along the spinal region occurs in seven progressive stages.

As shown in the drawing below, these 7 stages are marked by small wheel-like symbols called *chakras* or *lotus*, which the yogi "sees" and "feels" in different parts of his or her spinal area.

The color and position of the *chakra* that the yogi sees and feels, indicate his or her progress.[57]

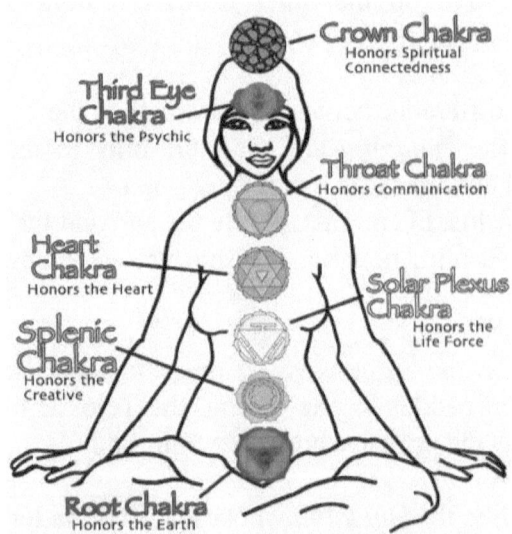

Fig. 4.1   The 7 positions of chakras

---

[57] "*The ancient yogis depicted the evolution of mankind, and the consciousness of the individual in particular, as a progression of seven steps. The seven centers have symbolic locations in the spinal column. These centers are referred to either as chakras or lotuses. Chakra means wheel and symbolizes the process of the movement of life. The chakras are best understood as levels of consciousness.*" Swami Sivananda Radha, "Kundalini: An Overview," in <u>Kundalini, Evolution and Enlightenment</u>, ed. John White (New York: Anchor Book, 1979), 48.

These 7 stages are:
(1) *Root Chakra* – Honors the Earth
(2) *Splenic Chakra* – Honors the Creative
(3) *Solar Plexus Chakra* – Honors the Life Force
(4) *Heart Chakra* – Honors the Heart
(5) *Throat Chakra* – Honors Communication
(6) *Third Eye Chakra* - Honors the Psychic
(7) *Crown Chakra* – Honors Spiritual Connectedness

These ascending *chakras* grant ascending levels of power. For example, the yogi who attains the 6th chakra (top left of picture) called the *Third Eye Chakra*, will receive the power to "see" the *auras* of other people.

When the 7th *Crown Chakra* (see top of picture) called the *Sahasrara* or 1000-petalled lotus is felt above the head center, then the *chakra* system within that person is complete. His or her *kundalini* has completely uncoiled and has risen to the top of the head. The yogi who has attained the Crown Chakra is said to possess pure consciousness and extraordinary capabilities.

The Sahasrara

> ...*is the most transcending and all-encompassing state of consciousness that can be experienced. There is nothing beyond this. The individual consciousness is* **merged** *with divine consciousness.*
> *... Gradually, through systematic practice, the yogi learns complete mastery of this energy and is able to direct it at will....*[58]

---

[58] Swami Rama, *Awakening,* 43-44. (Bold was added.)

In the *spirit*, during the 1ˢᵗ decade of my inner journey, I also saw tiny chakra-like starbursts that were always of one color. At other times, the figures were not starbursts but tiny circles, also of one color.

In the Telos, these tiny starbursts or circles appeared at will and were not triggered by what I did or did not do.

While praying in church, sitting in our living room, taking a slow walk or doing whatever and I briefly closed my eyes, on the inner side of my forehead, one, two, and at rare times, three or more starbursts or tiny circles may appear, always of one particular color.

I did not feel energic sensations flowing out of these tiny figures that I saw, so they were not centers of consciousness like the *chakras*. The tiny figures that I saw at times, functioned more as *spiritual cues.* They seemed to guide me about the rightness and wrongness of my actions and thoughts, through their colors.

Because these usually appeared after kindly actions or decisions I've made, I associated the tiny *digital blue* figures that I saw, with right choices and healing. *Reddish* and the dull *yellowish-green figures* seemed to relate to poor diet and poor health. When I received those, I ate healthier, exercised more and slept longer. At rare times, I saw soft *white* or *gold* starbursts or circles which I associated with spiritual gains.

One difference between the *chakras* and the Telos is, that the ascending levels of higher consciousness of the *chakras* can only be attained through use of yoga techniques; so, these phenomena are matter. *Chakras,* which are matter, will die when the person dies; while our *spirit* lives on even after we die.

A 2ⁿᵈ difference is, the Crown Chakra is said to "*merge*" with the divine. In this book and in my experiences, the Telos, which is "earthly *spirit,*" does *not* ever become divine or "merge" with the divine. Only God, who was not created, is called *divine*.

3. AURAS

"*Auras* " are emanations of colors that outline a person's body, and which enlightened yogis are supposedly able to "see."

A book of fiction, *The Third Eye: The Autobiography of a Tibetan Lama,* published in 1956, popularized the fanciful belief that humans naturally exude *auras,* and that yogis who have attained the 6th *chakra* called the *Third Eye,* can infer a person's state of health, feelings, character and state of evolution by just looking at the colors and other characteristics of that person's *aura.*

The writer of that book of fiction, a plumber from England named Cyril Henry Hoskins, claimed that he would get visions and dreams in his reincarnation of a Tibetan Lama.

That popular book which he wrote under the pseudonym of T. Lobsang Rampa, explained that,

> People have **auras,** *coloured outlines which surround the body, and by intensity of those colours those experienced in the art can deduce a person's health, integrity, and general state of evolution.*[59]

and

---

[59] T. Lobsang Rampa, *The Third Eye: The autobiography of a Tibetan Lama* (New York: Doubleday and Company, Inc. 1957), 137. (Bold was added.)

> *... I could look at them and get the impression of their true thoughts, the genuine liking for me, the jealousy from some, and the indifference from others. It was not just a matter of seeing colors and knowing all; I had trained to understand what those colours mean.* (103)

I do not see *auras* in the Telos, but I have wondered about *after-images*.

It is common experience that when we stare at an object for a while and then close our eyes, an *after-image* of that object is retained on that inner side of our forehead where our dreams also appear. I have observed however, that the color of the *afterimage* of an object in the inner eye, is different from the color of that same object as seen with my naked eyes. This difference is intriguing.

Oftentimes in church with my eyes open, I may unconsciously be looking at the *red* dress or *red* shirt of the person praying in front of me. But when I briefly close my eyes, that dress or shirt is *green* in the *afterimage* that I "see" in my inner eye.

Conversely around December, with my eyelids open, I see the *green* of Christmas trees in the church. But when I close my eyelids, the same trees have a *reddish afterimage* in my inner eye.

Orange is seen as *blue* in the inner eye, and vice-versa.

In the ROYGBIV[60] spectrum of light, there is a 4-place displacement between the colors of objects as seen with our naked eyes versus the colors of its *afterimage* in our inner eye. *Red* is 4 spaces apart from *green*, in the spectrum of light. Similarly, *orange* is 4 spaces apart from *blue*.

---

[60] ROYGBIV stands for red, orange, yellow, green, blue, indigo, and violet.

I mention this 4-displacement difference between the colors of objects as seen with the naked eyes, versus the colors of their *afterimages* as retained in the inner eye, because this may help explain optical illusions.

4. CHI or QI

In 1997 when I was 55 years old, I attended a workshop on acupuncture. After the instructor pierced needles in my ear lobes, I was told to cup my hands over my ears and feel the heat that was released. The instructor called this released heat, *chi*.

He then made me place a hand over the ears of a younger woman in the workshop. I felt her *chi*, which was much stronger than mine.

This multifaceted force called *chi*, which has been studied and used by the Chinese in their martial and healing arts, has features that closely resemble the Telos.

For example, the Chinese physical exercise called Tai Chi teaches that the bodily movement of deeply inhaling the "good" *chi* and then exhaling the "bad" *chi*, has a calming and healing effect.

Telos also has that same calming and healing effect. When we offer up to God our worries, troubles, and other "bad" in our life circumstances with a contrite heart and sincere prayer, the doors of the Telos open and the *spirit* fills us with a calming, and healing effect that diminish our burden.

The *chi* and the Telos are also alike in that both are natural forces that do not discriminate. Both the *chi* and the *spirit* are available and "come" to everyone, seemingly at random and at no cost.

Where they differ is, the Telos or *spirit* is not tangible as heat. It cannot be pinpointed in parts of our body. And the Telos cannot be manipulated.

5. SUB-ATOMIC PARTICLES

At times, I while my time on my cell phone by going through the enthralling pictorials and write-ups about galaxies, quasars, dark matter, etc. in our expanding universe and about the infinitesimal protons, electrons, neutrinos and other sub-atomic particles on the qubits end.

Recent internet articles that I've read mention that as science sees further and further beyond our galaxy and is able to study ever smaller particles inside protons and neutrinos, our assumptions about reality itself will be *shifting*.

Not really. The difference between quantum mechanics and our expanding universe on one hand, vis-à-vis the Telos or *spirit* on the other hand, will always be that no matter what size, distance from earth, powers, and behaviors an object, event, power, or phenomenon may possess – if it *can* be studied, sensed, and manipulated by the human mind, gadgets, instruments, and techniques – then that substance, event, power, or phenomenon is *matter,* not *spirit*.

Intellectuals have this resolute quest to sense, capture, study, know, and manipulate the realm of the Telos or *spirit,* and even God Himself, but that **will not ever happen!** Realize that the minds of humans are merely like an atom in the planet called earth, while the Telos is the womb that holds, guides, sustains, nourishes, and nurtures the entire universe and everything in it.

The next chapter will describe the bizarre, awesome, and incredible "touch" of the Telos, as I have experienced it.

Chapter 5
WHAT DOES IT FEEL LIKE, TO BE "TAKEN" BY THE *SPIRIT*?

In these past 34 years, I experienced the "touch" of the Telos or *spirit* in these ways:

1. the *spirit* as **RAPTURE**

About two weeks after that wonderful episode of the strewn flowers on our walkway, described in chapter 3, I began to notice that the peaceful and energizing feeling from the strewn flowers, *was still in me*!

Unbeknownst to everyone, that spiritual and soothing peace remained and stayed in me, not for a day, or a week, or a month, but for about 5 years!

When I woke up, that spiritual "high," which I came to know as the *rapture*, was with me. Wherever I went, it went with me. Rain or shine or snow or storm, it stayed with me.

In the *rapture*, the feeling is one of elation, of being "raised high" and of even being "exalted." It is a "spiritual high" that cannot be mistaken for anything else.

In this year of 2021, as I look back to that episode on our walkway in the spring of 1987, 34 years ago, I need to caution that there are *two dangers* that come with that soothing feeling of peace called *rapture*.

The 1ˢᵗ danger is, when men, women, and children are blessed and wrapped in a cloud of energizing and peaceful spiritual "highs" for months and years, without guidance from church, science, or traditions, they can develop an *exaggerated and inflated sense of worth or power* called **inflation.** Like I did.

They may begin to fantasize that they have a special relationships to a deity. Or that they will soon receive special powers and capabilities. Or that they are destined to become famous.

If one is not careful, these inflated beliefs could harden into *delusions of grandeur,* and a woman may soon believe that she is the queen of England; a man that he is a famous songwriter; or that one is God's "chosen one" who will change humankind for the better.

A delusion of *grandeur, paranoia,* or of other kinds, can be *temporary,* like mine was, and was soon overcome. If the delusion becomes *permanent*, it is harder to cure.

The 2nd danger may occur after 3 to 5 years, when the *rapture* suddenly *ends forever*, without warning or explanation.

After 5 years of walking on air and floating on clouds, I not only got used to that spiritual "high" but also began to believe that I was favored by the divine for some great task. When my *rapture* suddenly ended without warning and there was no dream to explain why, I felt hurt, dislocated, and abandoned! *So, I was not favored after all?*

It took many years before I could accept that the *rapture* may have been intended as fat, to sustain the journeyer for the tough and rough challenges and struggles that were yet to come, and which did come!

This sudden stoppage of their *rapture* could have a personal and traumatic impact on some people. They may remain deeply offended or resentful for years and could pull away into temporary or permanent angry seclusion! Still others may feel ashamed or guilty that perhaps the *rapture* ended because they had done something wrong. Most commonly, in different parts of the world, many quietly and privately succumb to depression, distrust, paranoia, or anxieties!

If you are going through a phase of the *rapture,* be cautious, humble, and learn to sincerely pray. Be observant and keep a diary of what you are going through, so that you have something to read and mull about during your long journey. Trust your common sense and *do not be afraid.*

Reading good books is also helpful. I was greatly helped by the writings of Thomas Merton, Pierre Teilhard de Chardin, and Carl G. Jung. But I also enjoyed the fiction of Joseph Conrad, David Baldacci, David B. Coe, Fyodor Dostoyevsky, Ernest Hemingway, Dean Koontz, and numerous others, for these helped normalize my sense of day-to-day. Books give helpful insights about our humanity and are a helpful way of holding on to reality.

The Judeo-Christian Bible is the book that helped me the most. During the past 3 decades, when I slowly read it from cover to cover 3 or 4 times, from *Genesis* to *The Revelation*, my dream experiences slowly fell into place and slowly revealed their meanings to me, on their own.

It may have been during the 2nd and 3rd decades into my dream experiences when I began to discern that my evolutionary experiences in the *spirit* are guided by biblical **prophecies**. I'd get an insight here, a clue there, a dawning here, an experience there, an insight from something I'd read or from something that the priest had said in his homily at Mass. Bit by bit, I slowly understood that the universe itself and its workings can <u>only</u> be fully explained by *divine design and purpose*; <u>not</u> by mechanical means.

2. the spirit as **NUMEN**

I didn't hear the alarm clock, had woken up at 7am and realized that I would be late for work that day! But I fell asleep again into my 5th dream and experienced the life-changing healing "touch" of the *numen* in my 5th dream!

I woke up into my 5th dream, and as I watched 2 groups of small birds came together on the roof of a seminary-like building, from the tips of my toes to the tips of my hair as I lay sleeping, I felt the *numen* healing me of the heavy anxiety that I carried at the time.

When I got up, and ever thereafter, I didn't have that kind of anxiety ever again. Also thereafter, when I pray, most times the *numen* responds and capacitates me with trust, courage to cope, and the capacity to discern through the unusual events and phenomena in my life.

Often, the *spirit* as *numen* "comes" to a child, man, or woman who is falling apart because of deep distress, grief, or anxiety, and the *numen* will hold them together. Most people have also experienced the *numen* as a deeply religious *wrap of holiness and awe* when they are in deep meditation or prayer. Jung's vision of the Crucified Christ when he was 64 years old and which he said had "profoundly shaken" him, which is described in the next chapter, was a *numinous* experience.

All of us have the *numen* in our body cells. It is that attribute of the *spirit* that gives us the capacity to know God, to be truthful, humble, holy, brave, and free. It is that feeling of awe, deep reverence, fear, and dread, as though one is in the presence of God Himself, that some of you may have at times, experienced. It is a solemn *religious feeling* that is felt in the marrow of one's bones; even by those who have never prayed or who do not believe in God.

Unlike the *rapture* that comes and goes, the *numen* is that aspect of the *spirit* that is innate, indispensable, vital, permanent, and essential for the <u>normal</u> and <u>ongoing</u> human functioning and wellbeing of every human being. When the *numen* - our capacity to know God, to be truthful, humble, holy, brave, and free - is *repressed* or *blocked* from freely flowing within a person, he or she could suffer from severe anxiety neurosis for years.

In his autobiography, Jung described how he "cured" a female client who suffered from *severe anxiety neurosis* for years, by simply allowing her *numen* to flow in her again.

During the early period of his counseling with this client, Jung was guided *by his own dreams* to learn that her father and she as well, had *turned their backs to God* and no longer practiced their faith; but that she was the granddaughter of a Jewish Rabbi and *zaddik*.[61]

> *She had no mythological ideas, and therefore the most essential feature of her nature could find no way to express itself. All her conscious activity was directed toward flirtation, clothes, and sex, because she knew of nothing else.* She knew **only the intellect** *and lived a meaningless life. In reality she was a child of God whose destiny was to fulfill His secret will.* ***I had to awaken mythological and religious ideas in her,*** *for she belonged to that class of human beings of whom spiritual activity is demanded. Thus her life took on meaning, and* **no trace of the neurosis was left***. In this case I had applied no "method," but had sensed the* **presence of the numen.** *My explaining this to her had accomplished the cure. Method did not matter here; what mattered was the "fear of God".*[62]

In addition, since time began, the *numen* has endowed **people** with the holiness to become **saints, prophets, healers,** and **gurus**. Those people made holy, will have powers to *prophecy about the future* and to *heal people's bodily and emotional illnesses.*

The **numinous** powers endowed upon **that** person will forever remain **only** in that person, even after he or she has died. The numinous powers of saints, prophets, healers, and gurus cannot be usurped or transferred to others.

The *numen* also endowed **objects** like a tree or rock, or **places** where a *numinous event*, miracle, and other

---

[61] In medieval Jewish ethics, a *zaddik* was a morally perfected human being.
[62] Jung, *Memories,* 139-140. (Bold was added.) The whole chapter on *"Psychiatric Activities,"* pp.114 to 145 will be very worth your time to read.

religious phenomenon had actually and physically occurred, to become **sacred shrines**. A *shrine* is a holy and numinous **object** or **place** <u>where the divine abides,</u> and which has <u>numinous powers to heal</u> bodily and mental ills and disorders. The *shrine* can be a temple; church; mountain; river; cave; waterfall; tree; dried up riverbed; rock; a cathedral; the remaining walls of a ruined temple, and so on.

All religions have hundreds of *holy people* and *shrines*. Year after year, the sick, the old, the young, and the devoted go on pilgrimages, walk for miles, and even climb mountains to *physically* visit "their" sacred *shrines,* so they can *bodily* experience the *numinous nearness* of "their" gods and goddesses, and receive bodily and mental healings.

Hinduism's **Amarnath Cave** which is situated 14,000 ft above sea level in the Himalayas is an example of a *shrine*. In July to August of every year, from 400,000 to 600,000 pilgrims walk for 43 kilometers and climb up 14,000 ft above sea level to visit it.

Fig 5.1 Pilgrims on their climb to the Amarnath Cave

The Amarnath Cave is considered to be the abode of Shiva, Hinduism's God of Destruction and Reproduction who is also a member of the Hindu Trinity, and is Guardian of the Absolute.

The ancient Hindu text of Mahabharata mentions that Lingam[63] represents their Lord Shiva. For Hindus, Shiva is said to be enshrined in this cave in the form of an ice-lingam.

This picture below of an ice-lingam is a stalagmite that is formed due to the freezing of water drops that fall from the roof of the cave and grow upward vertically from the cave floor. Hindus worship it as the holy and numinous image of their Lord Shiva.

Fig 5.2 The Shiva Lingam at the Amarnath Cave Temple

---

[63] Lingam is a stylized phallic symbol of the masculine cosmic principle and of the Hindu God Shiva.

In Judaism, another ancient religion, their tradition for pilgrimages is, three times a year, all the Jewish people must appear before Yahweh their God in their holy city and *shrine* of *Jerusalem*, the place that their Lord God has chosen as "their" place of worship.

Their pilgrimages are made at the Festival of the Unleavened Bread **(Passover)**, the Festival of Weeks **(Shavuot)**, and the Festival of Tabernacles **(Sukkot)**.

The picture below shows the Jews during their celebration of Shavuot, the Festival of Weeks. They gather and worship inside the Wailing Wall, the remaining *shrine* from their Second Temple destroyed by the Romans in 70 A.D.

Fig. 5.3 Jewish people celebrating their festival of Shavuot inside their *shrine* of the Wailing Wall on Mt. Zion, in Jerusalem.

Shavuot is the time when Yahweh God commands His people the Jews, to give a freewill offering. Everyone is to bring something, giving in proportion to how God has blessed them. To the Jewish people, their holy places and *shrines* are innate and sacred to them.

3. the spirit as **NEMESIS**

It may have been five years into my dream experiences when I noticed that the Telos has a retributive attribute that punished me when I did bad and rewarded me when I did good. I named this trait the *nemesis*.[64]

Nemesis, this retributive attribute of the Telos, is similar to Hinduism and Buddhism's *karma*.[65] But in *nemesis*, the penalty is imposed *immediately* after the act!

In a way, *Nemesis* seems kinder because the offense is completely mended and atoned for during one's lifetime and the offender knows the offense that he is doing atonement for. Also, offenders do not pass on their social offenses as karma to their posterity. (Although the *karma* penalty is probably for more grievous offenses because the karmic stain is passed on from generation to generation.)

One other curious thing about the Telos' *nemesis* is, it is only concerned and it only enforces this one rule: *all people must* **deal fairly** *with* **others**, *at all times and in all ways*.

---

[64] *Nemesis* is the goddess of retributive justice or vengeance in Greek mythology.

[65] *Karma* is the force generated by a person's actions, that is held in Hinduism and Buddhism to be the motive power for the round of rebirths and deaths that a person will endure. The person must free oneself from the effects of karma before one can nirvana.

As I have experienced it, I was only immediately penalized when I was *unfair, unkind,* or *unjust* to others.

Nemesis also seems to require justice for all, not only for the poor, but also for the rich. Not only for the brown people, blacks, and red race; but also for the yellow and white people. Not only for the slaves, but also for the slave owners. *Nemesis* seems to require that everyone is to be good neighbor to everyone else, at all times, in all ways, and in all places,

During the 1st decade of my experiences in the *spirit*, I naively surmised that there are 2 sets of rules for our existence: a set of rules when in the realm of the *spirit*, and a separate set of rules for existence in the real world. Like a firewall of sorts or what is now called compartmentalized psychology.

So, when I was in my inner world and in the realm of the *spirit*, I was *good*. But because in the real world the goal is to win, I *bent the rules* a few times to have an edge over others in my work and in social interactions.

I was actually surprised that the *spirit* punished me when *I bent the rules a few times*, because the rules I bent seemed to me to be "small sins!" To make sure that I understood that there *is* a difference between right and wrong no matter how "small" it may be, when I bent the rules again in my favor, the *spirit* exacted *triple penalty* than what I had gained from bending the rules in my favor.

The first time it happened, I thought it was just a coincidence. On the 3rd time that I was walloped by the penalty that got even steeper, I got the message! This moral mandate of the *spirit* is *blind* and *impersonal justice*! Without exception, everyone must be fair to everyone else, in all places, under all circumstances!

I was shaken a few times to see that the *spirit* exacted very heavy penalties on people who've hurt me. I understood then, that the *spirit* imposes its own rules, over which humans have no control.

On the positive side, when people do good, the *spirit* as *nemesis* rewards people with joy, blessings, and prosperity. Not only to them and their children but throughout all the generations of their lineage. Perhaps the windfalls and good that come unexpectedly into our lives are the droppings and carry-overs, from the good that our parents and ancestors have done for others and our world.

4. *the spirit as* **BURST OF KNOWLEDGE**

If you've wondered why people who are "touched" by the *spirit* behave in curious and strange ways, I can vouch that it is because the *spirit* itself "touches" people in strange and bizarre ways. For one thing, the *spirit* itself manifests as hallucinations, "voices," trance, visuals, dreams, and as other outlandish and discombobulating forms!

I startle easily, so in these past 34 years, I was often jolted when without warning and without apparent trigger, these pictorials just appeared on my inner forehead when I briefly closed my eyes! The most disconcerting and also the most awesome mode that I experienced was when the *spirit* came as *bursts of knowledge.*

I received my first *burst of knowledge* while I was mindlessly washing dishes in the sink and briefly closed my eyes. My mouth dropped open in utter surprise when on that inner side of my forehead, a visual appeared! It showed a paper tape machine, like the one used to telegraph messages in the late 1800's!

The visual zoomed in closer so I could read the single-line sentences that were steadily printed by the tape machine. As this moving paper tape with the sentences printed on it slowly passed across my inner eye from right to left, I thought to myself, "*Whoa...what now?*" But I kept my eyes closed and my hands slowly settled the plate I was washing on the sink. The single-line sentences were describing great events from the past and the future, in astonishing scope and depth that were all-encompassing! These knowledge would have blown my mind had they not been explained so simply.

Even on first reading, I understood the correlations and importance of those events to us all! As I read on, I felt safer and was filled with joy that the secrets about our world, and about past and future world events, were *already known* to the *spirit!* In *this very spirit* that is in all of us!

I received *knowledge bursts* about half a dozen times, during the initial 5 to 6 years of my dream experiences. Each time, my mouth fell open and I was caught off-guard. Then afterwards, I was elated beyond words.

After a *knowledge-burst* had passed, I strongly resolved that the next time it happened, I would retain a phrase or word from those revelations, so I can share it with others. I placed pen and paper in the kitchen, living room, and in my pockets when I gardened or took a walk, so I can quickly jot down a word or phrase. However, when a *knowledge-burst* ended, I would be so rapt with awe at what were revealed! When I recovered moments later, the wonderment remained but I could not ever recall a single word of that knowledge.

Other people however, like Einstein, Beethoven and others, were able to grasp and hold on to a mathematical formula, tunes or melodies, and other forms of "bursts" that popped up in their consciousness.

Because of my few *knowledge bursts*, I am convinced that Jung must be right: *that there is a collective unconscious* in each and all people that holds *all* the memories of humankind's past as well as knowledge about humankind's future.[66] And sometimes, the *spirit* allows the person to get a glimpse of a few pieces of those knowledge.

Who knows? Perhaps Yahweh our Creator will endow the fully evolved humans of the future with biological structures that will enable them to access this vast knowledge stored in our collective unconscious *as needed*, and *whenever* they want to!

This skill will come in handy for those humans from Earth whom Elon Musk of Tesla foretells, may be living in the planet Mars by 2026 or shortly thereafter.

5. the spirit as **SUBLIMINAL**

In the early years of my spiritual experiences, I intermittently received a group of visuals that came in glossy, lacquered, and dark textures of brown, purple or forest green.

These visuals seemed "right there," at the borderline fringes of my consciousness; so I called them *subliminal*.

Those glossy visuals also appeared without warning when I briefly closed my eyes! They were not triggered by what I did or did not do.

Around Thanksgiving in 1990, while I was lounging on our sofa in the living room, I lightly closed my eyes and a short visual episode unfolded on my inner eye. This *subliminal* was in a monotone of darkened and glossy forest green, as though it was early evening.

---

[66] *Collective unconscious* as defined by Jung is described in chap 6 of this book.

From a far distance, the visual showed about 6 to 8 U.S. soldiers walking diagonally in single file. They walked from bottom-left to top right in the visual, on a terrain that I assumed was in Kuwait and the Gulf Zone because the 1st Gulf War was going on then.

As I watched, the last soldier broke away from the line, walked towards his left, and then knelt to examine a soft white light on the ground. The visual zoomed in to show that this light which the kneeling soldier was looking at, was flowing like a spring from the ground. This light was liquid in form and had the texture and solid whiteness of milk.[67] Then I felt wordless impulses in my body which translated itself into this thought: *"The Desert Storm war will be over soon."*

I opened my eyes and wondered what that was about.

Remarkably, the 1st Gulf War did end three months later, on Feb 28, 1991.

A few years later, in July 1993, I received another *subliminal*. It was also a complete surprise.

On that afternoon, I was seated by the window in our living room, engrossedly working on a term paper on the computer. It may have been around 2 or 3 pm.

My jaw dropped and my eyes widened as the top living profile of then U.S. President Bill Clinton briefly appeared on the screen of my computer!

I watched Mr. Clinton's side profile for a minute or two.

---

[67] This same white light in liquid form that had the solid whiteness of milk, appeared in my 8th dream as the Diamond Body. My 8th dream and the Diamond Body will be described with more details in my Book Two.

He was facing towards the right side of the computer, and it seemed as though I was actually watching him live. He was seated behind a desk, perhaps in some room of the White House at that very moment, but there were no decors or furniture around him to identify where he was. It was just him from his shoulders up. He moved his head slightly to his right, then to his left, a few times. He seemed pensive.

Then I must have blinked because his profile was gone, and I was again looking at my term paper.

A few days later, I read in the news that a close friend of Bill and Hillary Clinton, Vince Foster, had committed suicide on that day.

During the first 10 years of my dream experiences, I might have received a dozen or more of these glossy *subliminals*, but I don't get them anymore. A few times, they showed different groups of people doing the usual day to day activities. One *subliminal* showed a group of friends - black American young adults - chit chatting on their stairway area. Another showed a Caucasian family casually gathered and talking on the patio of their home. A few times, I saw meadows with tall grass blown by the wind. One time, I saw grounds that were covered with small pink flowers; another time, the grounds were covered with small blue flowers.

S*ubliminals* did not seem to have any direct and personal bearing on me or my families. They seemed to be sample experiences of how, in the future, fully evolved humans will probably have the capacity to *bypass* the dimensional barriers of time and space, and in the realm of the *spirit,* actually "see" events as they are simultaneously happening, in other geographic places! *Wouldn't that be awesome?*

6. *the spirit as* **FOREBODING**

I saved this attribute of the *spirit* for last because I find it distressful and oftentimes frightening.

Forebodings are dreams or visuals that hint of *ill-happenings* that may come to oneself, family members, or friends.

People who have received a *foreboding* become anxious about having dreams. A female friend had told me that years ago she had very graphic dreams that *forebode* her father's medical condition, which did come true. Since then, she shudders and dreads having dreams.

In *forebodings*, as I have experienced it, symbols have *specific* and *set meanings*.

In my forebodings, a *car* symbolizes *a male adversary*. In my past visuals, a *car* about to crash against my car, and another car about to hit me and so on, were followed by adverse life events involving *male* participants.

In one visual, the car coming towards me but did not hit me, as I was standing by an open but walled bridge area, was a *foreboding* about a *male* foster teen-ager whom I was then counseling, who lied against me and cost me my job.

On another occasion, I briefly closed my eyes and had a visual that showed a *jeep* driving away, which suddenly turned right towards the highway and drove away. It was a *foreboding* that the male Russian contractor who reneged and refused to complete the paid-for improvements to be done in our house in Jersey City, would go scot free; and he did!

A few dreams I had that showed *cats*, also seemed to forebode adverse events about to happen, bad luck of some sorts. So, in real life, even until now, when a *cat* walks across the road where I'm driving, I would turn back or park and wait until another car drives through and breaks that cat's bad omen. Then I say a prayer before I slowly drive on.

Whenever I sense that a *foreboding* is about to show, whether I'm half-awake and half-asleep in the early mornings or deep in sleep at night, I would use my hand to force my eyes to open, so that I do not see the rest of the dreaded something-to-happen. Sometimes that worked but most times not. The *foreboding* presented itself again in a dream or visual anyway. What I found helpful is to say a prayer for protection from harm over and over, and not to dwell on it too much. It's not mechanically guaranteed, but prayers *can* and *do* help soften and ward off forebodings.

For those who are now going through their *second birthing,* know that these kinds of awesome, bewildering and uncanny incursions of the *spirit* into our consciousness and life events just described in this chapter, *will happen a lot* during the early 10 to 15 years of one's evolutionary journey. Document them simply and truthfully, to help you understand what you are going through.

In my case fortuitously, when I was terminated from work in June 1992, five years after my dream experiences began, on the advice of a parish priest I had applied for acceptance to a 2-year graduate Pastoral Counseling program at Loyola University in Chicago. With his help and recommendation, I was accepted.

The psychology and theology courses I took at Loyola, under good teachers and with fine classmates, were timely and helpful. They provided the concepts, theories, discussions and interactions that guided my feet, my heart, and my soul during the early part of my inner journey.

One of my courses at Loyola during the 1st semester was an *Introduction to the Theories of Carl G. Jung*. This course and the 9 or 10 books from Jung's *Collected Works* which I later read, reread, and reread at the Skokie library, were tremendously providential. Jung's writings and theories gave me concepts and tools which, like a shepherd's staff, I walked with and leaned on throughout my journey and *2nd birthing*.

Part III, which now follows, describes the life, research and theories of Carl G. Jung, this humble and great man who *discovered,* named, and documented the special group of dreams and instincts that are evolving humankind to their state of wholeness.

Part III
Jung's Paradigm of Individuation

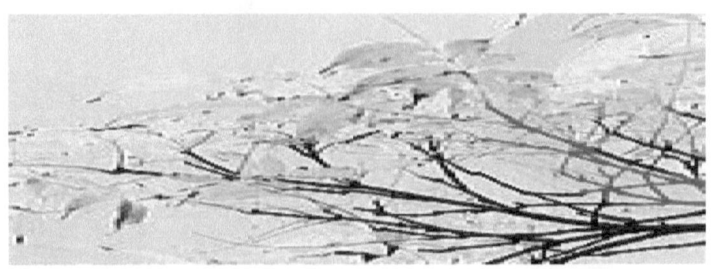

When people say I am wise, or a sage, I cannot accept it. A man once dipped a hatful of water from a stream. What did that amount to? I am not that stream. I am at the stream, but I do nothing. Other people are at the same stream, but most of them find they have something to do with it. I do nothing. I never think that I am the one who must see to it that cherries grow on stalks. I stand and behold, admiring what nature can do.

There is a fine old story about a student who came to a rabbi and said, "In the olden days there were men who saw the face of God. Why don't they anymore?" The rabbi replied, "Because nowadays no one can stoop so low."
One must stoop a little in order to fetch water from the stream.

The difference between most people and myself is that for me the "dividing walls" are transparent. That is my peculiarity. Others find these walls so opaque that they see nothing behind and therefore think nothing is there. To some extent I perceive the processes going on in the background, and that gives me an inner certainty. [68]

---

[68] Carl G. Jung, <u>Memories, Dreams, Reflections</u>. Rev. Ed. (New York: Pantheon Books, 1972), 355.

Chapter 6
Who was Carl G. Jung?

Fig. 6.1 Jung living a simple life

Carl Gustav Jung [1875-1961] was born in Kesswil, Switzerland.

At age 25, he completed his studies in psychiatry and began his tenure as a psychiatrist at Burgholzli Psychiatric Clinic in Zurich.

Five years later, at 30, he was promoted to senior psychiatrist at the Clinic and was also a Lecturer in psychiatry at the University of Zurich.

His autobiography, <u>Memories, Dreams, Reflections</u>, describes his personal experiences relating to the unconscious; his friendship and collaboration with Sigmund Freud for 5 years; and absorbing details about his life, research, clinical cases, and theories. For those who want to know more about their own inner world and how dreams transform people, his autobiography is very worthwhile reading.

Jung was a serious reader across many disciplines and languages. His father, Paul Achilles Jung, a Protestant minister who also studied languages, began giving him lessons in Latin soon after he was six. Jung spoke German, French, English, and Italian and could read Sanskrit, Greek, and some Aramaic.

As a child, he loved the illustrations of Brahma, Vishnu and Shiva - the Hindu trinity.[69] He used to pester his mother Emilie Preiswerk, to read out loud from books about Hinduism and other religions. He remained interested in myths and religions and drew on these traditions to enlighten him in his work and in formulating his theories.

Jung was also inquisitive about current cultures, beliefs, and ways of life. In 1913, when he was 38 years old, he visited places in Italy. In 1920, he traveled to North Africa, in the Moorish soil of Tunis, Algiers and the oasis city of Tozeur in the Sahara. On his second trip to the U.S., he visited the Pueblo Indians of New Mexico. Then he visited Kenya and Uganda in Africa in 1925. He also traveled to places in India, Ceylon, and to Ravenna in Greece.[70]

In 1903, when Jung was 28 years old and a psychiatrist at the Burgholzli Psychiatric Clinic, together with students and associates, a few of whom were Americans, he set up a laboratory for experimental psychopathology to investigate

---

[69] In the Hindu religion, *Brahma* is the absolute primordial essence; the supreme soul of the universe, self-existent and eternal, from which all things emanate and to which all things return. *Vishnu* is a major deity, known to have many incarnations, of which the most famous is as Krishna. *Shiva* is the god of destruction and reproduction.

[70] Jung, *Memories*, 238-288. This chapter on "Travels" in his autobiography describes Jung's impressions about the places that he visited and the people he met in those travels.

disturbances in word association.[71] In this research, a patient was given a stimulus word, e.g., *"rain,"* and was asked to immediately respond with the first word or thought that comes to mind, like *"tears," "fun," "storm," "cleansing"* or other associative words.

If the patient takes a long time to respond, hedges, or cannot give a reply, these reactions were noted. The delay or hesitation may indicate that the stimulus word had stirred a *psychic disturbance* in the patient; perhaps a past trauma or an unacceptable inclination that he or she had *repressed* and wanted to forget. Further investigation usually revealed that the repressed trauma or inclination was the cause or had contributed to the patient's *neurosis*.[72] Freud studied repression as revealed in *dreams* while Jung studied repression as revealed in his *word association* method. This comparability of their studies about repression got Jung interested in Freud's work.

> *What chiefly interested me was...* [Freud's] *application to dreams of the concept of the repression mechanism .... This was important to me because I had frequently encountered* **repressions** *in my experiments with word association; in response to certain stimulus words the patient either has no associative answer or was unduly slow in his reaction time. As was later discovered, such a disturbance occurred each time the stimulus word had touched upon a* **psychic lesion** *or* **conflict**. *... My reading of Freud's* The Interpretation of Dreams *showed me that the repression mechanism was at work here, and that the facts I had observed*

---

[71] *"My real scientific work began with the association experiment in 1903. I regard it as my first scientific work...."* Ibid., 201.

[72] *Neurosis* is a mild form of mental disorder that is triggered when the Telos or unconscious is repressed. Its symptoms include anxiety, obsessions, compulsions, or phobias. A neurosis is less severe in form and prognosis than a psychosis.

were consonant with his theory. Thus I was able to corroborate Freud's line of argument. (Jung, 147) (Bold and word in parenthesis were added.)

The circumstances that brought Jung and Freud to later meet and become friends was an academic congress in Munich in 1906, where a lecturer discussed Freud's theory of obsessional neurosis but did not give Freud due credit. At that time, the academic world had not yet accepted Freud's sexual theory. Freud was so unpopular that his name was not allowed to be mentioned in academic conferences.

...Freud was definitely persona non grata in the academic world at the time.... "Important people" at most mentioned him surreptitiously, and at congresses he was discussed only in the corridors, never on the floor. (148)

But Jung felt that not giving credit to Freud for his obsessional theory was not right. He took the side of Freud and published articles in which he defended Freud's theories about obsessional neurosis; then he sent copies of his articles to Freud.[73]

After correspondence between the two began, Freud subsequently invited Jung to visit him in Vienna. They first met in March 1907, when Jung was 31 and Freud was 50. Friendship was immediate.

---

[73] *"The first breakthrough* [for Freud] *came in 1906, when Jung, then principal psychiatrist at the renowned clinic Burgholzli in Zurich, sent Freud an offprint. Freud responded promptly; a cordial correspondence blossomed, and the friendship was cemented by Jung's visit to Freud in early 1907."* Gay, Peter. "Sigmund Freud: A Brief Life" in *The Future of an Illusion,* Sigmund Freud(New York: W.W. Norton and Company, 1989), xvi. (Words in brackets in this footnote quote were added for clarity.)

> *We met at one o'clock in the afternoon and talked virtually without a pause for thirteen hours. Freud was the first man of real importance I had encountered; in my experience up to that time, no one else could compare with him. ... I found him extremely intelligent, shrewd, and altogether remarkable.* (Jung, 149)

But even in that happy first meeting, Freud's extreme obsession about sexuality left a negative impression on Jung.

> *There was something else that seemed to me significant at that first meeting. It had to do with things which I was able to think out and understand only after our friendship was over. There was no mistaking the fact that Freud was emotionally involved in his sexual theory to an extraordinary degree. When he spoke of it, his tone became urgent, almost anxious, and all signs of his normally critical and skeptical manner vanished. A strange, deeply moved expression came over his face....* (150)

Meanwhile, Jung's American associates in his word association research had published articles about it in American journals. As Jung became known in the circles of psychiatry in the U.S., many Americans traveled to Switzerland for therapy and counseling with Jung.[74]

When Jung was invited to lecture at Clark University in Massachusetts in 1909, independently, Sigmund Freud was invited as well. Jung and Freud traveled as friends by ship to America. Both were given honorary degrees by this

---

[74] *"The association experiment and the psychogalvanic experiment were chiefly responsible for my reputation in America. Very soon many patients from that country were coming to me."* (Jung, Memories, 120)

university. Sigmund Freud delivered his Five Lectures on Psychoanalysis; Carl Jung lectured on the association method and the psychology of childhood.

As their friendship deepened, Freud frequently alluded to Jung as his successor.

> *Jung was prominent in the first international congress of psychoanalysts at Salzburg in the spring of 1908, and was appointed, the following year, editor of a newly founded Yearbook. Freud, delighted with Jung, anointed him his son, his crown prince.... Hence, when the International Psychoanalytic Association was founded in March 1910, in Nurnberg, Jung was Freud's logical, inevitable, choice for President.* (Gay, xvii)

Freud's sexual theory, however, stood in the way of their collaboration and friendship. When Jung expressed his concern that Freud's sexual theory would morally degrade the current societies and spiritually debauch the culture of the generations to come, Freud did not care. This bothered Jung.

> *Wherever, in a person or in a work of art, an expression of spirituality ... came to light... [Freud]... insinuated that it was **repressed sexuality**. Anything that could not be directly interpreted as sexuality, he referred to as **"psychosexuality."** I protested that this hypothesis, carried to its logical conclusion, would lead to an annihilating judgment upon culture.* ***Culture would then appear as a mere farce, the morbid consequence of repressed sexuality.*** *"Yes," he assented, "so it is, and that is just a curse of fate against which we are powerless to contend." I was by no means disposed to agree or to let it go at that....*

(Jung, 149-150) (Bold and word in brackets were added for clarity.)

One conversation stuck in Jung's mind.

> *I can still recall vividly how Freud said to me, "My dear Jung, promise me never to abandon the sexual theory. That is the most essential thing of all. You see, we must make a dogma of it...."*
>
> *It was the words "bulwark" and "dogma" that alarmed me; for a dogma... is... to suppress doubts once and for all. But that no longer has anything to do with scientific judgment; only with personal power drive.*
>
> *This was the thing that struck at the heart of our friendship. I knew that I would never be able to accept such an attitude.* **To me the sexual theory was just as occult,** *that is to say,* **just as unproven an hypothesis, as many other speculative views.**
>
> ....
>
> *Sexuality evidently meant more to Freud than to other people.* (Jung, 150-151) (Bold were added for emphasis.)

In 1911, Alfred Adler, who also disagreed with Freud's sexual theory, left Freud's group.[75] The following year, Jung also left Freud's group.

> *When then, Freud announced his intention of identifying theory and method and making them into*

---

[75] *"But Adler was developing distinctive psychological ideas, which featured* **aggressiveness** *over sexuality, and "organ inferiority" as a dominant cause of neuroses. A split became inevitable, and, in the summer of 1911, Adler and some of his adherents resigned, leaving Freud and the Freudians in control of the Vienna Society."* Gay, xvii. (Bold in this footnote quote was added.)

> some kind of dogma, I could no longer collaborate with him; there remained no choice for me but to withdraw.
>
> When I was working on my book about the libido and approaching the end of the chapter "The Sacrifice," I knew in advance that its publication would cost me my friendship with Freud. For I planned to set down in it... various other ideas in which I differed from Freud. ... I knew he would never be able to accept any of my ideas on this subject. (167)

All the three psychoanalysts, Freud, Adler, and Jung – were in agreement that a repressed unconscious is the *cause* of neuroses; but they disagreed on what is the <u>nature or basic drive of the unconscious,</u> and what is the <u>treatment for neurosis</u>. In the early 1900's, psychoanalysis split up into 3 directions.

Since for Freud, the nature of the unconscious is **sexual**, the prescribed Freudian cure is for the person to pursue and fulfill his or her sexual needs and fantasies using reasonable ways and means.

Since for Adler, the nature of the unconscious is **aggressiveness** and desire for **power**, the prescribed Adlerian treatment and cure for neurosis is for the person to pursue, within reason, his or her desire for power.

Since for Jung, the nature of the unconscious is **religio**us, developing oneself according to the guidance and nurturance of the unconscious or *spirit* is the suggested cure for the person's neurosis.

In 1912, five years into his friendship with Freud, Jung published his book <u>Transformations and Symbols of the</u>

Libido,[76] where he set down his own theories about the libido and the unconscious that differed from Freud's. As Jung had anticipated, his book ended his friendship and collaboration with Freud. By that time, Freud was popular. The Vienna circle of psychoanalysts, who were Freud's friends and close associates, declared Jung's book to be "*rubbish*" and Jung "a *mystic.*" Jung resigned from the Vienna group in 1914.

Jung now 37, suddenly found himself alone and on his own.

> *After the parting of the ways with Freud, a period of inner uncertainty began for me. It would be no exaggeration to call it a state of disorientation. I felt totally suspended in mid-air, for I had not yet found my own footing.* (170)

A year later, while on a journey by himself, Jung was "seized" by a vision which lasted for one hour. It showed thousands of drowned bodies in a sea of blood! This vision, which was repeated, so overwhelmed Jung that he thought he had a psychotic episode.

> *In October* [1913], *while I was alone on a journey, I was suddenly seized by an overpowering vision.... I saw... the drowned bodies of uncounted thousands. Then the whole sea turned to blood. This vision lasted about an hour.*
>
> *Two weeks passed; then the vision recurred... even more vividly than before, and the blood was more emphasized. An inner voice spoke. "Look at it well; it*

---

[76] This book was originally written in German and translated into English in 1956 as <u>Symbols of Transformation</u>, vol. 5 of Jung's <u>Collected Works.</u>

is wholly real and it will be so. You cannot doubt it." (175) (Word in brackets was added for clarity.)

Because of those two visions and the many dreams and visuals that he was also receiving, two months after his visions of the seas of blood, Jung decided to confront his unconscious before it overwhelmed him. While sitting on his desk, he allowed himself to "drop" into his inner world. This was the beginning of his self-analysis.

It was during the Advent of the year 1913 – December 12, to be exact- that I resolved upon the decisive step. I was sitting at my desk once more, thinking over my fears. Then I let myself drop. Suddenly it was as though the ground literally gave way beneath my feet, and I plunged down into dark depths. I could not fend off a feeling of panic. But then, abruptly, at not too great a depth, I landed on my feet in a soft, sticky mass. I felt great relief.... (179)

Jung's narrations of what he encountered on his drops into his unconscious have to be read in Jung's own words,[77] to get a feel of the breadth and depth of his tremendous familiarity with ancient symbols. After his initial drop, he used the same method for getting back into his inner world.

In order to seize hold of the fantasies, I frequently imagined a steep descent. ... The first time I reached, as it were, a depth of about a thousand feet; the next time I found myself at the edge of a cosmic abyss.

---

[77] His chapter on *"Confrontation with the Unconscious"* is on pp 170-199 of his autobiography.

Wherever he landed, he interacted with the fantasy figures that he "met" on that level, as though they were real people. To keep his experiment scientific, he carefully documented his interactions and impressions about fantasies.[78]

So that he would not become disoriented and fall prey to his fantasies, he differentiated himself from the "contents" of his unconscious by giving the fantasy figures names, based on the characteristics they manifested. He named one fantasy figure *Philemon*,[79] and another, *Siegfried*.[80]

He credited the fantasy figure that he named Philemon, as the *guru* or teacher who helped him understand that his unconscious was <u>different from</u> and a <u>superior</u> realm of intelligence, to his mind.

> *Philemon represented a **force which was not myself**. In my fantasies I held conversations with him.... He said I treated thoughts as if I generated them myself, but in his view thoughts were like animals in the forest, or people in a room.... "If you should see people in a room, you would not think that you had made those people, or that you were responsible for them." It was he who taught me **psychic objectivity**, the reality of the psyche. Through him... I understood that there is something in me which can say things that*

---

[78] "*I wrote these fantasies down first in the Black Book; later, I transferred them to the Red Book, which I also embellished with drawings.*" (180)

[79] Philemon may be in reference to an aged and poor man in Greek mythology who with his wife Baucis treated a disguised Zeus hospitably, and were rewarded by Zeus with a splendid temple.

[80] Siegfried was a hero in a Germanic legend who slayed a dragon guarding a gold hoard and woke up Brunhild from her enchanted sleep.

I do not know and do not intend, things which may even be directed against me.

Psychologically, Philemon represented superior insight. ...I went walking up and down the garden with him, and to me he was...a **guru***.* (183) (Bold were added)

His drawing of Philemon with wings like an angel, as kept in the Red Book, is shown below. Jung mentioned that in his fantasy wanderings, a *large black snake,* also shown lower-right in this picture, often appeared.

Fig 6.2 Jung's drawing of Philemon

In myths [Jung explained,] *the snake is a frequent counterpart of the hero. There are numerous accounts of their affinity. For example, the hero has eyes like a snake, or after his death he is changed into a snake and revered as such, or the snake is his mother, etc. In my fantasy, therefore, the presence of the snake was an indication of a hero myth.* (182) (Words in brackets mine.)

In August 1914, ten months after his visions of the seas of blood and while he was on his 2nd year into his self-experiment, World War I broke out! Jung realized then that his visions of the seas of blood were a *foreshadowing* of World War I [1914-18], in which 32 countries were involved and 37 million people had died.

Jung's self-experiment which began in December 1913, lasted until 1917.

In 1922, ten years after his break-up with Freud, Jung and his wife Emma bought a piece of land by a lake. On it, Jung, now 47, built a house of stone which he designed from his childhood dream. They lived a simple life, without running water and electricity. Jung chopped the wood, cooked the food, lit the lamps, and fetched water from the well.[81]

He had given up his professorship at the University of Zurich and his psychiatric work at the Burgholzi Clinic, but he continued to see his clients which had increased over the years. His clientele now included some Americans, including John D. Rockefeller's daughter.

> *Just to be closer to him, John D. Rockefeller's daughter Edith relocated from New York to Zurich bringing her children, their personal tutor, a*

---

[81] *"These simple acts make man simple, and how difficult it is to be simple."* (200)

physician, governess and private secretary with her. She stayed for almost seven months.[82]

In the next 18 years and thereafter, in this house by the lake where he also built a personal library, Jung focused on his theories and research.

To Jung, his 4 years of self-experiment from 1913 to 1917, were the most important years of his life! While he was *"inside the magic mountain,"* his unconscious imposed a message upon him with overwhelming force.

> *... it seems as though a message had come to me with overwhelming force. There were things in the images which concerned not only myself but many others also. It was then that I ceased to belong to myself alone, ceased to have the right to do so. From then on, my life belonged to the generality.* (192)

To comply with the task that his unconscious had imposed upon him,

> *... I took great care to try to understand every single image, every item of my psychic inventory, and to classify them scientifically – so far as this was possible – and, above all, to realize them in actual life. ...* **The images of the unconscious place a great responsibility upon a man...** *(193)* (Bold were added)

---

[82] Quoted from *Londonstressmanagement.com/studies in psychotherapy/Jung.html*, in Google.

From his experiences "*inside the magic mountain*" and his interactions with his fantasy figures, Jung had observed that the fantasy figures in his dreams and visuals had *similar* traits and characteristics as the personages in the different literature, folk tales, religions, and myths of the cultures of the world.

He also noted to his

> ... *amazement that European and American men and women coming to me for psychological advice were* [also] *producing in their dreams and fantasies symbols* **similar to**, *and often* **identical** *with, the symbols found in the mystery religions of antiquity, in mythology, folklore, fairy tales....*[83]

To explain ***why this was so***, that heroes, saints, and other personages from the ancient past *can appear in people's dreams at any time,* even into the modern times and in any place of the world, Jung boldly came up with the original insight and theory that the life experiences of each and all people across the ages and into the present and future times, **must be continually recorded in an *infinitely vast realm of memories* that exists in every human being**. He named this vast memory in people, the ***collective unconscious***.

As he conceived it, Jung's **collective unconscious**:
1. exists in **everyone**;
2. contains people's past and present **memories**
3. and glimpses of the near **future**;

---

[83] C.G. Jung, "Prefatory Note" to <u>Psychology and Alchemy</u>, CW Vol. 12, 2nd ed. (New Jersey: Princeton University Press). (Bold was added for emphasis.)

4. participates in the ongoing evolution of humans **into spiritual beings**; and
5. this ongoing evolution of humans into spiritual beings are happening through the guidance of a **special group of dreams and instincts** that he had studied in great detail.

Jung's theories, which were drawn from his own experiences and personal transformations, were verified by the similar experiences and personal transformations of his hundreds of clients. But Jung felt, that in order for his theories to be scientific and valid, he had to find objective confirmation from *other* sources.

In their house by the lake, Jung undertook a total of 18 years of research to find validation from *other* sources, for his two groups of theories.

I. The 1st group of theories he wanted to validate was, that there is a *collective unconscious* which exists in each and all people, [84] **and this realm of intelligence is ongoingly transforming the human individual into a spiritual being.**

> ... *I was led to postulate a* ***"collective unconscious"*** *...of an activity in the human psyche making for the* ***spiritual development*** *of the individual human being.*[85]

---

[84] *"The collective unconscious is common to all; it is the foundation of what the ancients called the "sympathy of all things."* (Jung, Memories, 138)

[85] C.G. Jung, "Prefatory Note" to *Psychology and Alchemy*, CW Vol. 12, 2 ed. (New Jersey: Princeton University Press). (Bold was added for emphasis)

It took 8 years of research, but he found corroboration of his 1st group of theories in the Gnostic writings.

Gnosticism was a movement in the 2nd century by a group of Christian sects, who searched for higher enlightenment by combining Christian teachings with ideas from Greek and oriental philosophies.

This Gnostic teaching quoted below, that a vessel called *krater,* filled with spirit, was sent by God to endow people with higher consciousness and spiritual renewal, corroborated Jung's 1st group of theories that there is a *collective unconscious* in people that participates in the development of humans into spiritual beings.

> *In the writings of Poimandres, a pagan Gnostic, the* **krater** *was a vessel filled with spirit, which the creator-god sent down to earth so that those who strove for higher consciousness might be baptized in it. It was a kind of uterus of spiritual renewal, and corresponded to the alchemical vat in which transformation of substances took place.* (Jung, MDR, Footnote on 201)

II.. The 2nd group of theories he wanted corroborated by other sources, were his theories that the transformations of people into spiritual beings, were happening through the action and guidance of a special group of dreams and instincts.

It took 10 more years of research, but he also found corroboration for his 2nd group of theories in the writings of the *alchemists.*

The alchemists were searching for the *secret* in the heart of matter that can transform base metals into gold, cure all diseases, and prolong human life; in the same way that modern scientists now search for the God particle by smashing atoms in giant atom colliders. The alchemists codenamed that *secret*, the *philosopher's stone* or *lapis lazuli*.

The alchemists cooked and boiled mixtures and combinations of substances and chemicals in vats over many decades, then they documented their processes and its outcomes and discoveries in intricately coded metaphors which took Jung 10 years to decode. But after Jung could read their coded metaphors, Jung found a sturdy correlation between the processes used by the alchemists in their search for the *lapis lazuli*, and his 2nd group of theories about a special group of dreams and instincts that evolve the beliefs, worldviews, and behaviors of people, himself and his clients included, into spiritual beings.

After his combined 18 years of research that corroborated his 1st and 2nd groups of theories by other sources, Jung formulated and consolidated both groups of discoveries and theories into his **Paradigm of Individuation**.

> *Only after I had familiarized myself with alchemy did I realize ... that the psyche is transformed or developed by the relationship of the ego to the contents of the unconscious. In individual cases that* **transformation can be read from dreams and fantasies.** *... Through the study of these collective transformation processes and through understanding of alchemical symbolism I arrived at the central concept of my psychology: the process of* **individuation**. (209) (Bold were added)

At 52, with his 1st and 2nd groups of theories corroborated and consolidated into his *Paradigm of Individuation*, Jung felt that everything had fallen nicely into place.

> *This was, of course, a momentous discovery. I had stumbled upon the historical counterpart of my psychology of the unconscious. The possibility of a comparison with alchemy, and the uninterrupted intellectual chain back to Gnosticism gave substance to my psychology. When I pored over these old texts everything fell into place: the fantasy-images, the empirical material I had gathered in my practice, and the conclusions I had drawn from it. (205)*

But 12 years later, when he was 64, Jung felt that something was still "missing" in his formulations. Primarily because the alchemists never found the *philosopher's stone* or *lapis lazuli*, that *secret* in the heart of matter that can transform base metal into gold, cure all diseases, and give eternal life to humans.

Secondly because in the past, Jung's important decisions and directions in life were *always corroborated* by his unconscious. It has been 12 years since he completed and consolidated his theories into his Individuation Paradigm. His unconscious *should already* have sent him a confirmation of some kind.

Shortly after, in that same year of 1939, when he was 64, Jung received a vision of the Crucified Jesus.

> *One night I awoke and saw, bathed in bright light at the foot of the bed, the figure of Christ on the Cross. It was not quite life-size, but extremely distinct; and I saw that his body was made of **greenish-gold**. The vision was marvelously beautiful, and yet I was **profoundly shaken** by it.* (211) (Bold was added)

His vision revealed to Jung that the Crucified body of Jesus *is* the alchemists' *Philosopher's Stone* or *Lapis Lazuli!* Christ's *greenish-gold* body on the Cross *is* the **secret** *in the heart of matter* that can cure all diseases, grant immortal life, and transform people into spiritual beings!

This corroboration from the unconscious that his theories and Paradigm of Individuation were on the right track, touched Jung deeply.

He wrote,

> *The vision came to me as if to point out that I had overlooked something in my reflections.... When I realized that the vision pointed to this central alchemical symbol, and that I had had an essentially alchemical vision of Christ, I felt comforted.* (210-11)

Chapter 7
NOTES ABOUT JUNG'S PARADIGM OF INDIVIDUATION

The reader might ask: *Why is it that very few people know about Jung's Individuation Paradigm?*

The answer is because as of today, there is as yet no single piece of writing that contains the *pieces, sequence,* and *entirety* of the different stages of transformations of Jung's Individuation Paradigm.

My Book Two, entitled <u>8 Dreams and the Diamond Body,</u> planned for publication in late 2023, will be the first published book that will name the stages of his Individuation Paradigm; the names, characteristics, and powers of the dream symbols and instincts that guide the transformation at every stage; and the perils to avoid at these stages.

How did that happen, *that Jung's Paradigm of Individuation, his magnum opus, is nowhere written?*

The stages of Jung's personal transformations and the similar transformations in his clients, from which he gained the insights and theoretical discoveries that he made, did not happen all at once. They spanned a period of over 50 years.

As Jung experienced the transformations wrought in himself by his dreams and visuals and as he discovered similar processes and transformations in his clients, he wrote about *that* particular piece of his findings and discoveries, and published it, at *that* particular period in time!

The descriptions of the stages of his own transformations and those of his clients, which became the stages of his Individuation Paradigm, are therefore not described in its entirety in any one book; they are *scattered* in the 18 volumes of his <u>Collected Works</u> and other writings.

To date, no one really knows the **entirety** of Jung's individuation paradigm or what its **stages** are.

Some Jungian psychoanalysts and theorists have popularized a few of the special dream symbols that trigger transformations in people, like the *shadow* and the *anima-animus*. But the other dream symbols and stages of his individuation paradigm have remained unknown.

It is also difficult to determine the **sequence** of the stages of transformation in Jung's paradigm; as to what stage comes first, second, and so on; because except for a few scattered hints here and there in his 18 volumes of <u>Collected Works,</u> the **sequential correlations** of the stages of his paradigm are *not* specified anywhere in his writings.

In my Book Two, I am able to specify with certainty that Jung's Individuation Paradigm has *8 stages* and I also name with certainty what these stages are, because I received the stages of Jung's Paradigm as my series of 8 dreams from 1987 to 1993! Their *sequential order*, as well, was defined to me by the order in which those 8 dreams came. And the Telos guided me to live out the meanings, perils, and outcomes of these 8 stages, in these past 34 years and still continuing.

However, it was my former professor at Loyola, Prof. Robert Sears, S.J., who should get the credit for doing the essential work of years of readings and research, and then identifying, collecting, and then sequencing 5 of the 8 stages of Jung's paradigm into an outline. I received a copy of Prof Sears' outline when I took his *Introductory Course to Jung's Theories* in my freshman year.

Prof. Sears' outline gave his students 5 of the stages of Jung's individuation paradigm as well as their sequence. That is why when I wrote my term paper for his class at the end of that 1st semester at Loyola, I was able to see the correlation between the stages of Jung's paradigm and my 8 dreams; how they matched outright, *like a hand into a glove*. Guided by the Telos and related life experiences, I later added 3 more of the stages to Prof. Sears' outline.

Prof. Carl Meier, a past president of the Jungian Institute, emphasized that it is *"probably impossible"* to find any human development that fully matches Jung's paradigm, but it did happen to me. His comment is shown below:

> *I must emphasize one point: it is **probably impossible** to find a development such as that described in the many examples given by Jung for what he calls the individuation process, unless it is somebody who lives his personal myth. This means a person who goes along with the process, in such a way as to stimulate this process and this development by*

> *taking an active part in it, which is to show an interest that is properly called religious.*[86]

It is important to clarify that I had received my series of 8 dreams from the early spring of 1987 to late summer of 1993, years and months *before* Loyola was in my purview. My 8 dreams, visuals, visions, etc. and related experiences were *not* in any way, stimulated or induced by Jung's theories.

But as though by design, soon after my termination from work as a Systems Project Manager at an insurance company in Northbrook, Illinois, I was accepted to the two-year Pastoral Counseling graduate program at Loyola University in Chicago. In a fortuitous way, because I lost my job, I was able to attend school full-time. My children took part-time jobs while in school and we coped as well as we could with our strained finances, even as our lives were re-arranged in unforeseen ways.

In this Pastoral Counseling graduate program at Loyola, 12 students are selected every year from among applicants from different parts of the U.S. and from different countries of the world. The selected 12 students attend the *same classes*, with a few electives, during those two years. They get to know and bond with each other and grow from their interactions and sharing of experiences and insights.

During those two years at Loyola, the interactions with my classmates and professors, and the psychological and theological concepts, theories, and techniques I was learning, enabled me to gain a foothold into my inner world.

---

[86] Carl A. Meier, *Soul and Body: Essays on the Theories of C. G. Jung* (San Francisco: The Lapis Press, 1986), 149.

It was because of my studies at Loyola and my extra readings, that I found the words and language to describe the unusual and mystifying dreams, impulses and other extra-sensory phenomena I was undergoing.

The course that helped me the most was the *Introductory Course to Jung* under Prof. Robert Sears, S.J.

In the first few weeks of listening to Prof Sears' lectures and from reading Jung's books, I learned that there are not one, but *two* realms of intelligence in us: our *consciousness,* which I later called the mind, and the *unconscious,* which I later called the Telos or *spirit.*

I was intrigued to learn that our dreams come from the unconscious; and that our dreams have functions and purpose. Knowing little about dreams and our unconscious, these learnings were eye openers that enabled me to see my strange experiences in a new light.

Jung's writings and his own experiences into his inner world, were like a road map that enabled me to find my bearings. Also, just knowing that another person, Carl Jung, had gone through what I was going through, *normalized* my experiences. What a relief that was!

The deep well where I was climbing remained dark and unknowable but the insights and observations of Jung, this great man, who had trodden through his inner world, were like small stepping stones wedged into the walls, that I held on to. As I continued to climb, I felt liberated.

From reading Jung and as I paid more attention to what was going on inside me, I came to understand that at night while we sleep, whether we are aware of it or not, dreams enter our inner world to nurture and replenish our body systems and minds. This is the work of our *ordinary* dreams.

The exciting part was Jung's descriptions that an *extraordinary* group of dreams and instincts that have the power to change attitudes, worldviews, and how people function and behave, are also at work in us! Unbeknownst to us, Jung wrote, we are *all* being transformed in a natural way into *new beings* by our dreams.

> *There are natural transformation processes which simply happen to us, whether we like it or not, and whether we know it or not. ... [These] Natural transformation processes announce themselves mainly in dreams.*[87]

He explained further that some dreams trigger a

> *... long-drawn process of inner transformation and rebirth into another being. This 'other being' is the other person in ourselves – that larger and greater personality maturing within us....*[88]

I was so heartened by Jung's writings.

His observations and theories which coincided with my inklings that my dream experiences were kind of transforming me in some ways, were comforting. Whenever parts of his writings matched aspects of my experiences, I said to myself, *Ah, he had trodden here before me*; and I felt reassured.

When I wrote my term paper at the end of that introductory course, I didn't yet know what my dreams were

---

[87] C.G.Jung, *Four Archetypes*, extracted from *The Archetypes and the Collective Unconscious*, Vol. 9, part 1, of the Collected Works of C.G.Jung. (New Jersey: Princeton University Press, 1973), 64. The word in brackets was added for continuity.

[88] Ibid, 64-65.

about, what I was going through, or where I was going. I was greatly surprised and incredibly flattered to discover that the symbols, impulses, and transformations described in the stages of Jung's Paradigm of Individuation *perfectly matched* my series of 8 dreams.

Jung's great service to humankind was that he conscientiously studied, named, documented in detail, and gave many anecdotal examples of the how, why, when, and the where, of these metamorphic processes that are transforming humans into spiritual beings. Then he consolidated his theories into his Paradigm of Individuation.

My own contribution is my 8 dreams and my related transformational experiences in the past 34 years, which will be described in great detail in my Book Two.

BIBLIOGRAPHY

Campbell, Joseph, ed. *The Portable Jung.* New York: The Viking Press, 1974.

Camus, Albert. *The Myth of Sisyphus and Other Essays*, translated by Justin O'Brien. New York: Vintage International, 1983.

Editorial Staff of Life. *The World's Great Religions.* New York: Golden Press, 1967.

Freud, Sigmund. *Beyond the Pleasure Principle.* New York: W. W. Norton & Company, 1961.

Freud, Sigmund. *The Future of an Illusion.* New York: W. W. Norton & Company, 1961.

Gay, Peter. "Sigmund Freud: A Brief Life," *The Future of an Illusion*. Sigmund Freud. New York: W.W. Norton and Company, 1989.

Hall, Calvin S. *A Primer of Freudian Psychology.* New York: The New American Library of World Literature, Inc., 1961.

Jung, Carl G. *"Four Archetypes."* Extracted from *The Archetypes and the Collective Unconscious,* Vol. 9, Part 1 of the Collected Works of C. G. Jung. New Jersey: Princeton University Press, 1973.

Jung, Carl G. *Memories, Dreams, Reflections*, Rev. Ed. New York: Pantheon Books, 1972.

Jung, Carl G. "Prefatory Note" to *Psychology and Alchemy*, Vol. 12 of CW. 2nd ed. New Jersey: Princeton University Press.

Jung, Carl G. *Psychology and Religion: West and East*, Vol. 11 of CW, New Jersey: Princeton University Press.

Jung, Carl G. *Psychological Types,* Vol 6 of CW. New Jersey: Princeton University Press.

Jung, Carl G. *The Archetypes of the Collective Unconscious.* Vol 9, Part I of CW. New Jersey: Princeton University Press, 1969.

Jung, Carl G. *Two Essays on Analytical Psychology*, Vol. 7 of CW, 2nd ed. New York: Pantheon Books.

Lawson, James Gilchrist. *Deeper Experiences of Famous Christians.* Ohio: Barbour Publishing, Inc., 2000.

Meier, Carl A. *Soul and Body: Essays on the Theories of C. G. Jung.* San Francisco: The Lapis Press, 1986.

Merton, Thomas. *Conjectures of an Innocent Bystander.* New York: Image Books, 2009.

Merton, Thomas. *The Seven Storey Mountain.* New York: Harcourt, Brace and Company, 1948.

Radha, Swami Sivananda Radha. *"Kundalini: An Overview."* in *Kundalini, Evolution and Enlightenment*, edited by John White. New York: Anchor Book, 1979.

Rahner, Karl. *Visions and Prophecies.* New York: Herder & Herder, 1963.

Rampa, T. Lobsang. *The Third Eye: The Autobiography of a Tibetan Lama*. New York: Doubleday & Company, Inc., 1957.

Rama, Swami. "The Awakening of Kundalini." in *Kundalini, Evolution and Enlightenment*, edited by John White. New York: Anchor Book, 1979.

Stevenson, Leslie. *Seven Theories of Human Nature*. New York: Oxford University Press, 1978.

Teilhard de Chardin, Pierre. *Hymn of the Universe*. New York: Harper & Row, 1965.

Teilhard de Chardin, Pierre. *Man's Place in Nature*. New York: Harper & Row, 1973.

Teilhard de Chardin, Pierre. *The Phenomenon of Man*. New York: Harper & Row, 1959.

www.ingramcontent.com/pod-product-compliance
Lightning Source LLC
LaVergne TN
LVHW091556060526
838200LV00036B/863